Freefall

Michael West

in collaboration with
The Corn Exchange

Methuen Drama

Published by Methuen Drama 2010

1 3 5 7 9 10 8 6 4 2

Methuen Drama
A & C Black Publishers Limited
36 Soho Square
London W1D 3QY
www.methuendrama.com

ISBN 978 1 408 13331 6

A CIP catalogue record for this book is available from
the British Library

Typeset by MPS, A Macmillan Company
Printed and bound in Great Britain by
CPI Cox & Wyman, Reading, Berkshire

Caution

The Corn Exchange production of

Freefall

By Michael West in collaboration with the company
Directed by Annie Ryan

Cast:	FREEFALL premiered in Project
Andrew Bennett A	Arts Centre Dublin as part of
Janet Moran B	the Ulster Bank Dublin Theatre
Ruth McGill C	Festival 2009, with Louis Lovett in
Declan Conlon D	the role of D
Damian Kearney G	
Paul Reid J	

Director Annie Ryan
Set Designer Kris Stone
Lighting Design Matt Frey
Composer Conor Linehan
Costume Designer
Debbie Millington
Sound Designer Ivan Birthistle
Tour Lighting Adrian Mullan
Video Designer Jack Phelan
Producer Sarah Durcan
Associate Producer Áine Beamish

Production Manager Lisa Mahony
Stage Director Mags Mulvey
Stage Manager Clare Howe
Photographer Richard Gilligan
Graphic Design Aad

*New Plays from Europe Festival
Wiesbaden, Germany June 2010 /
Galway Arts Festival July 2010 / UK
Premiere, Traverse Theatre, Edinburgh
Fringe Festival August 2010 / Festival
Cervantino, Mexico October 2010 /
The Abbey Theatre November 2010 /
National Tour 2011*

About the company

The Corn Exchange was founded in Dublin 1995 by Annie Ryan to explore various techniques of physical theatre. The main focus of the work is ensemble-based improvisation and a renegade form of Commedia dell'Arte, which came via chinese whispers from Mnouchkine's Théâtre du Soleil to LA's Actors' Gang to New Crime in Chicago to Dublin.

The Corn Exchange consists of a loose ensemble of players who engage in an ever-evolving practice. The company's work has toured throughout Ireland and to Australia, USA, UK, France, the Netherlands, Germany and Mexico.

The Corn Exchange provides professional training for actors, and for businesses through its unique leadership programme. The Corn Exchange's associate companies are Randolf SD | The Company and THISISPOPBABY.

The Corn Exchange is funded by The Arts Council of Ireland, Dublin City Council and Culture Ireland and by its Friends.

Acknowledgements & Thanks

Arts Council of Ireland, Culture Ireland, Dublin City Council, The Corn Exchange Board of Directors, Project Arts Centre, Dublin Theatre Festival, Abbey Theatre, Traverse Theatre, Galway Arts Festival, Studio Aad, Dr. Jill Bolte Taylor, Anne Bogart and SITI Company, Irish Theatre Institute, Theatre Forum, Trinity College Dublin, Mermaid Arts Centre, The Lab.

David Keating, Una McKevitt, Yvonne O'Reilly, Dick and Pat Ryan, Kathy Scott, Jonathan Wheeler, John and Cecily West, Thomas and Oliver West, Frank and Toni Durcan, Éamon Little, Paul Reid, Louis Lovett; Scott Burnett and Johnny Kelly at Aad, Wayne Jordan and Randolf SD | The Company, Jenny and Philly at THISISPOPBABY, Fiach Mac Conghail at the Abbey Theatre, Eugene Downes, Christine Sisk and Madeline Boughton at Culture Ireland.

Thank you also to those who do not wish to be credited.

Corn Exchange Associate companies:

Randolf SD | The Company   THISISPOPBABY
Gare St. Lazare Players

The Corn Exchange Theatre Company Ltd. The Priory Building, John Street West, Dublin 8, Ireland | *Tel:* +353 (0)1 640 1580 | *Web:* cornexchange.ie | *email:* hello@cornexchange.ie

Work to Date

Cultural Shrapnel
Dublin Fringe Festival 1995

Streetcar
DFF 1996 (winner Sexiest
Show of the Fringe 95)

Big Bad Woolf
DFF 1997

A Play on Two Chairs by Michael
West - DFF 1997 and national
and international tour

Baby Jane
Project Arts Centre 1998

Car Show
DFF 1998, national and UK
tour (winner Spirit of the
Fringe 1998, Judges' Prize
Irish Theatre Awards 1998
and Observer's Top Ten 2000)

The Seagull translated by
Michael West -Project Arts
Centre 1999

Foley by Michael West
UnFringed, Belltable, Limerick
2000, national tour, UK tour
2001, USA tour 2003

Lolita adapted by Michael West
co-production with Abbey
Theatre (winner Best
Supporting Actress and Best
Costume Design Irish Times
Irish Theatre Awards 2002)

Mud by María Irene Fornés,
2003 (Winner Best Production
Irish Times Irish Theatre
Awards 2003)

Dublin By Lamplight by Michael
West in collaboration with the
company - Project Arts Centre
2004, national tour 2005,
UK and International tour
2007 (winner Best Ensemble,
Edinburgh Stage 2005, Argus
Angel Brighton Festival 2007)

Everyday by Michael West in
collaboration with the company
Dublin Theatre Festival 2006
and national tour

Cat on a Hot Tin Roof by
Tennessee Williams, Dublin
Theatre Festival 2008

Freefall by Michael West in
collaboration with the company
Dublin Theatre Festival 2009
(winner Best New Play, Best
Director, Irish Times Irish
Theatre Awards 2009)

A maker's note

We set out to make what would become FREEFALL in late Autumn 2008, just as the world's markets collapsed. We knew that we wanted our new piece to be contemporary and to explore ways of theatrical transformation, deepening the style and practice of the company. When the fall happened, it became clear that change would become not just our means of telling our story, but the story itself.

In the face of change — even a change for the better — the psyche panics and resists. We want to know Who We Are, to be fixed as an identity. With each day, each year, the self we think we know passes away and another slightly different one takes its place. You could argue that your mental health depends on how well you deal with this never-ending process — these little deaths of the self. And after a while, we realised we were really making a piece about grief.

Not long after we started our research, we came across an extraordinary talk on ted.com by Dr. Jill Bolte Taylor, an American neuroscientist who suffered a catastrophic stroke yet recovered to tell her story. Her experience was one of profound desolation and despair, coupled with awareness and bliss, having lost the language centre that connects our sense of identity to our past and future. It helped enormously that she was already a happy-go-lucky gal from the Mid-West in the best brain hospital in the United States, but crucially, that she had a loving mother who climbed into bed with her and nursed her from infancy to adulthood again — who taught her how to eat, to sit up, to talk, to remember. She literally loved her back to adult-hood. It took eight years. Hers is an amazing, uplifting, American story.

So we thought, what if something like that happened to an ordinary Irish man? We knew he couldn't have quite the happy ending of Dr. Jill Bolte Taylor, but despite the lack of support he might have, there was still something at the core of our exploration into character that was about acceptance, humour and ultimately compassion.

As our man's story began to unfold in the summer, The Ryan Report was released after a nine-year investigation into the systemic rape and abuse of 30,000 children in the care of Catholic orphanages and industrial schools in Ireland, stretching back to the 1930s. Stories poured into the airwaves and newspapers, on the streets, in our rehearsal rooms. Ireland was overwhelmed with grief and remorse. It broke. It fell to its knees. Amidst job losses, the unknown future, the change in status, in life-style, this report was a shocking reminder of everyone's roots.

Our play isn't overtly about the collapse of the Celtic Tiger or the Catholic Church, but it is our setting — Ireland 2009. Ours was the attempt at finding the human experience within all this confusion, corruption, darkness and denial. While we found this incredibly sad story

on our hands, we also had the funniest actors you can imagine in the room. Irish actors are renowned for their playfulness and they are more or less allergic to sentimentality. And anyway, our ethos has always been one that works hard for precision, but at the end of the day, would do anything for a good gag.

This tension between rigour and play is very much at the core of what we do. Our company's name comes from an idea of creating an exchange of physical theatre techniques that empower the ensemble to make theatre. Our process has evolved to include an hour of yoga followed by voice training and ensemble work, after which we rehearse. The commitment to this practice greatly deepened our sense of appreciation for each other and the work. And the quality of this gratitude and flow infiltrated the story itself and made the production what it is.

Our expertise, if anything, is to shape the present moment for you to feel something. Change is our subject for this play, but it is also our method and at the very heart of the art form itself. Theatre seeks to transform space, to transform you. And then it's gone. You can't put it on a shelf, on a wall. It is experienced and then reverberates in you, as a memory. Perhaps we, who deal with the live form and ultimately its passing, might have a chance at capturing the sense of impossibility we all feel about our own passing, about change, the loss of ourselves as we grow and the anticipation of what might happen next.

Annie Ryan
Dublin, June 2010

Biographies

Michael West - Writer
Freefall is the third such collaboration with The Corn Exchange, following Dublin By Lamplight and Everyday. Other writing for the company includes Foley, performed by Andrew Bennett; Lolita, a co-production with the Abbey; and The Seagull. He has translated or adapted many texts, including The Marriage of Figaro (Abbey); The Canterville Ghost for the English National Ballet; Jean-Pierre Siméon's Stabat Mater Furiosa, performed in Avignon last year; and an acclaimed version of Death and The Ploughman which has been directed by Christian Schiaretti of the TNP in Lyon, and Anne Bogart for SITI company in the USA. He is currently writing the libretto for an opera by Jürgen Simpson. Freefall won the Irish Times Irish Theatre Award 2009 for Best New Play.

Annie Ryan - Director
Annie Ryan is the Artistic Director of The Corn Exchange, which she founded in Dublin in 1995 to engage Irish actors and theatre-makers in the ensemble-based physical theatre practices from her hometown, Chicago. She has directed all the company's work to date. Annie has also directed for the Ark Cultural Centre for Children, the Gate and the Abbey Theatre. Annie teaches The Corn Exchange's techniques of ensemble-based physical theatre and Commedia dell'Arte to professional actors, young people and corporate clients throughout Ireland as well as in Europe, the UK, the US and for the Maisha Film Lab in Kampala, Uganda. She has performed in theatre, television and film in the US and Ireland and is currently developing films with the company.

Andrew Bennett
Andrew's previous work with The Corn Exchange includes Cat on a Hot Tin Roof, Everyday, The Birthday Party Show, Lolita, Streetcar, Big Bad Woolf, Car Show, The Seagull and Michael West's one-man play, Foley. Other theatre includes: A Month in the Country, Fool for Love, Homeland, The Importance of Being Earnest, The Playboy of the Western World (national and US tour), Translations, The House, Good Evening Mr Collins, Sour Grapes, The Electrocution of Children, The Marriage of Figaro, Tarry Flynn, Saint Joan, The Rivals, The Map Maker's Sorrow and Tartuffe (the Abbey and Peacock Theatres); Oedipus Loves You (Pan Pan), The Playboy of the Western World (Druid), The Tinker's Curse and Conversations On A Homecoming (Livin' Dred), Family Stories (b*spoke), Beckett's Ghosts, What Where, Medea Material, Early Morning (Bedrock), Landscape with Argonauts, The Spanish Tragedy, The White Devil (Loose Canon), We Ourselves (Passion Machine), Words of Advice for Young People (Rough Magic) and Mac-Beth 7 (Pan-Pan). Film and television: Savage, Zonad, Garage, Prosperity, The General, David Copperfield, Alaska, Little White Lies, This Is Night Live, Pure Mule, The Clinic, Proof, Paths to Freedom, Salt Water, Angela's Ashes, Trí Scéal, Pentecost by Peter McDonald, and Your Bad Self (RTÉ).

Damian Kearney
Freefall is Damian's debut with The Corn Exchange. Theatre: The Comedy of Errors and The Resistible Rise of Arturo Ui (the Abbey Theatre), Troilus and Cressida (Cheek by Jowl), Someone to Watch Over Me (Manchester Library), Goldfish in the Sun (Everyman, Cork), The Tempest, Losing Steam (Corcadorca), The Romans in Britain (Crucible, Sheffield), A Whistle in the Dark (Glasgow Citizens), Translations (Manchester Library), The Lonesome West (New Vic, Stoke), The Cavalcaders (Lyric, Belfast), Hamlet, Julius Caesar, Love in a Wood (Royal Shakespeare Company), The Memory of Water (RSC Fringe) and Antigone (Old Vic/Donmar Warehouse). Film and television: The Tudors, Insatiable, The Wind That Shakes the Barley.

Declan Conlon

Declan appeared in Cat on a Hot Tin Roof for The Corn Exchange. Other theatre includes The Sanctuary Lamp, The Last days of a Reluctant Tyrant, A Whistle in the Dark, Famine, The Patriot Game, The Burial at Thebes, The Recruiting Officer, The Crucible, Julius Caesar, A Month in the Country, (for which he won a best supporting actor award at the Irish Times theatre awards), True West, All My Sons Henry IV part 1 (Abbey Theatre, Dublin); The Importance of Being Earnest, The Book of Evidence (Gate Theatre, Dublin); Improbable Frequency, Copenhagen (Rough Magic, Irish Times Theatre Award nomination best actor) Miss Julie (Landmark); As You Like It, The Spanish Tragedy, La Lupa, The Mysteries and Henry VI The Battle for the Throne, (RSC); The Walls, The Ends of the Earth and The Machine Wreckers, (National Theatre, London). Other UK theatre includes Macbeth (West End) and Our Country's Good (Young Vic). Television: Single Handed, Raw, The Tudors, Trouble in paradise, Proof, Any Time Now, Bachelors Walk, Dangerfield, and The Family. Films: Hereafter directed by Clint Eastwood, Trouble with Sex, Honest, All Souls Day.

Ruth Mc Gill

Ruth graduated from the Professional Acting Programme at the Samuel Beckett Centre, Trinity College Dublin. Her theatre work includes Freefall and Cat on a Hot Tin Roof (The Corn Exchange), Christ Deliver Us, The Last Days of a Reluctant Tyrant and The Cherry Orchard (Abbey Theatre), Macbecks (Olympia), Everybody Loves Sylvia, Fewer Emergencies, The Drowned World, The Illusion, Eeeugh!topia (Randolph SD | The Company), All in the Timing (Inis Theatre), The Turn of the Screw (Storytellers), Can You Catch a Mermaid? (Pavilion), Sweeney Todd (Gate Theatre), Woyzeck (Rough Magic Seeds) and The Shaughraun (Albery Theatre, London). Ruth is also a trained soprano and has co-devised and performed three cabaret shows with her company, Songspiel: Songspiel (Cobalt Café), Neues Songspiel (Bewleys Café) and Songspiel – Still Unplugged (Cobalt Café). Film and Television credits include Leap Year and The Clinic.

Janet Moran

Janet's previous work with The Corn Exchange includes Everyday, Dublin by Lamplight, and Car Show. Theatre: The Recruiting Officer, The Cherry Orchard, She Stoops to Conquer, Communion (nominated Best Supporting Actress at the Irish Times/ ESB Theatre Awards), The Barbaric Comedies, The Well of the Saints, and The Hostage (the Abbey Theatre); Unravelling the Ribbon (Guna Nua), Translations (Ouroboros), Submarine Man (Upstate), The Rep Experiment: Metamorphosis/Platanov, King Ubu (Galway Arts Festival), The Crock of Gold and Emma (Storytellers), Stella by Starlight (Gate Theatre), All's Well That Ends Well (CSI), Dancing at Lughnasa (An Grianan Theatre), Royal Supreme (Theatre Royal Plymouth), Guess Who's Coming to the Dinner (Calyspo), Dead Funny (Rough Magic), Playing From the Heart (The Ark), and Othello and Romeo and Juliet (Second Age). Radio includes The Eamon Lowe Show for Today FM. Film and television: Looking for Benji, Breakfast on Pluto, Love is the Drug, The Clinic, Fair City, Butcher Boy, Career Opportunities, Moll Flanders, and Nothing Personal.

Kris Stone - Set Designer

Kris Stone's designs have been seen throughout Europe and the United States in over 150 productions. Previous work with The Corn Exchange includes Everyday, Dublin By Lamplight (Dublin, Edinburgh & tours), Lolita (The Abbey) and Mud (Project Arts Centre). World Premier Off Broadway Credits include: A Lifetime Burning (Primary Stages – NYC), What Once We Felt (Lincoln Center – NYC), God's Ear (Vineyard & New Georges at CSC), and Cool Dip (Playwrights Horizon – NYC). Kris' designs chosen for the past Prague Quadrennial were Equivalents (Project Arts Centre, Dublin) and Iphigenia At Aulis (The San Jose Rep). She is currently included in a exhibition at The New York Public Library for the Performing Arts called "Curtain Call: Celebrating a Century of Women Designing for Live Performance." Kris studied at the Slade School of Fine Art in London, holds a BFA from the Art Institute of Chicago, an MFA from The Yale School of Drama in Stage Design. She has taught stage design at Vassar, NYU's Tisch School, Swarthmore, and Fordham University.

Conor Linehan - Composer

Conor's previous work with The Corn Exchange includes Everyday and Dublin by Lamplight. His work at the Abbey Theatre includes scores for The Last Days of a Reluctant Tyrant, Only an Apple, Marble, The School for Scandal, Homeland, The Cherry Orchard, The Tempest, She Stoops to Conquer, The Wake, Saint Joan, The Colleen Bawn and Love in the Title. Other theatre work includes The Cordelia Dream, The Taming of the Shrew, Macbeth, Two Gentlemen of Verona, Edward the Third, Loveplay, Luminosity (RSC), Peer Gynt, The Playboy of the Western World (National Theatre, London), American Buffalo, A View From the Bridge, Long Day's Journey Into Night (Gate Theatre), The Crock of Gold, Antigone (Storytellers), Mermaids (CoisCéim), Rebecca (David Pugh Ltd), Rosencrantz and Guildenstern are Dead, Four Knights at Knaresborough (West Yorkshire Playhouse), Tartuffe, Intemperance, The Mollusc, The Mayor of Zalamea (Liverpool Everyman), Carthaginians, A Doll's House (The Lyric, Belfast) and Twelfth Night (Thelma Holt Productions). Conor has written many scores for radio. In addition he works extensively as a concert pianist and has performed with all of Ireland's major orchestras, as well as performing extensive solo and chamber music repertoire. He recently toured the United States with the Dublin Philharmonic performing concertos by Beethoven and Shostakovich. Conor is on the piano faculty of the Royal Irish Academy of Music.

Matt Frey - Lighting Designer

Matt has also designed Dublin By Lamplight and Cat On A Hot Tin Roof with Corn Exchange. Other recent work includes, This Wide Night with Naked Angels, Melissa James Gibson's This at Playwrights Horizons, Heidi Schreck's Creature with P73 and New Georges, and Happy Now? at Primary Stages all in NYC. Other credits include: Brooklyn Academy of Music, Ridge Theater Company, The New Group, Manhattan Class Company, New York Theatre Workshop, Theatre for a New Audience, Soho Rep, as well as many other theatres in the US and internationally.

Debbie Millington - Costume Design

Debbie graduated from NCAD in 1997 with a degree in Fashion and Textiles. From there Debbie launched a career in fashion, designing her own label ladies wear collection. Debbie has worked in costume and set design in London, Sydney, Rio de Janeiro, Vancouver and Dublin – assisting on projects for television, commercials, music videos, events, festivals, theatre, dance and film. Costume design for theatre includes: Elements (Samuel Beckett Theatre) and Falling out of Love (Project Arts Centre), directed by John Breen and Red Light Winter written by Adam Rapp and adapted by Kelly Ruth Mercier in Vancouver, Canada.

Jack Phelan - Video Artist
Jack completed an MSc in Multimedia Systems in TCD in 2005 and currently works as a video & technology designer. Recent theatrical productions include MedEia (Corca Dorca), Love and Money (Hatch Theatre), The Shawshank Redemption (Lane Productions), Three Sisters (The Abbey Theatre), Little Gem (Gúna Nua), Woman and Scarecrow (The Peacock), and Macbeth (Siren Productions).

Sarah Durcan - Producer
Sarah holds a BA in Communication Studies from Dublin City University and a MA in Cultural Policy and Arts Management from University College Dublin. She has also worked in tourism and heritage management, entertainment and PR. Sarah joined The Corn Exchange Theatre Company in 2002. As producer and international promoter she produced Mud, Dublin by Lamplight (Dublin, national and international tours), The Birthday Party Show, Everyday in the Dublin Theatre Festival, Cat on a Hot Tin Roof in the DTF and national tour 2008, and the world premiere of Freefall in the DTF 2009.

Áine Beamish - Associate Producer
Áine has studied in Ireland and the U.K. and holds an MA in Cultural Policy and Arts Management from UCD and a B.A. in Digital Media. She has worked in production co-ordination and stage management with theatre companies throughout Ireland, including the Gate Theatre Dublin, Project Arts Centre, Andrews Lane, Everyman Palace, the Helix, the International Dublin Theatre Festival, Festival of World Cultures, Dublin Fringe Festival and St. Patrick's Festival. Áine is also Producer with Randolf SD | The Company who are hosted by The Corn Exchange, and is also producing a new documentary theatre piece by Úna Mc Kevitt called 565 + in the International Dublin Theatre Festival in 2010.

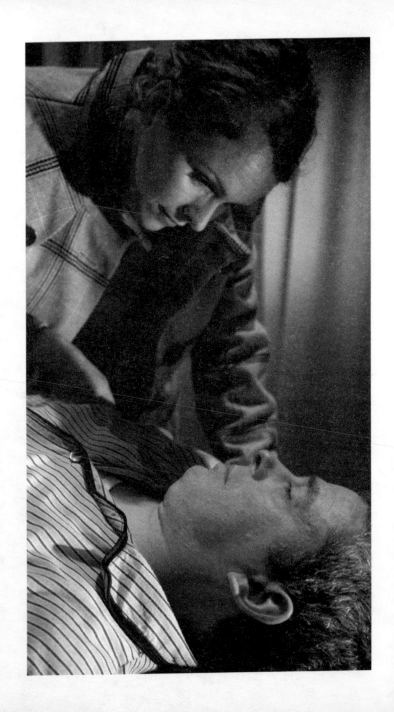

Take a bow!

The arts really matter to us in Ireland; they are a big part of people's lives, the country's single most popular pursuit. Our artists interpret our past, define who we are today, and imagine our future. We can all take pride in the enormous reputation our artists have earned around the world.

The arts play a vital role in our economy, and smart investment of taxpayers' money in the arts is repaid many times over. The dividends come in the form of a high value, creative economy driven by a flexible, educated, innovative work force, and in a cultural tourism industry worth €2.4 billion directly a year.

The Arts Council is the Irish Government agency for funding and developing the arts. Arts Council funding from the taxpayer, through the Department of Tourism, Culture and Sport, for 2010 is €69.15 million, that's less than €1 a week for every household.

So, at the end of your next great theatre performance, don't forget the role you played and take a bow yourself!

Find out what's on at
www.events.artscouncil.ie

You can find out more about the arts here:
www.artscouncil.ie

Michael West

Freefall

A writer's note: The Naming of Parts

The playwright Tom Murphy has said that a play is a theorem which the actors try to prove in front of an audience.

Our initial efforts to understand the geometry of *Freefall* involved four characters around a table, A, B, C and D. We knew they made up two couples AB and CD; and we knew that the story would in some way map the distance between a husband and wife – or as it's known in Euclidean notation |AB|.

As A moved to the centre of the whole thing, it made sense that everyone else would double up as the significant others in his life. To keep the book-keeping simple the roles were identified by letter rather than character name. The number of performers at one stage grew to seven, comprising five actors and two live musicians who were to take on small roles. Along the way the musicians were recorded playing Conor Linehan's achingly beautiful score and we let the actors tell the story. But a legacy of their existence is the absence of the letters E and F in the cast list.

All of which is proof of a kind that artistic collaboration is as much about what is left out as what stays in.

This is particularly the case in our play, for although the character A is all over the script, it seemed right that our main character should remain unnamed. It quietly underlined his anonymity and unassuming nature, and it felt like a correct and entirely natural fit. For it to work, it had to slip by without drawing attention to itself; it gave a certain pleasure to think that someone would only notice they were missing such a crucial piece of information considerably after the fact – that it would create a tiny lack, a hesitation, a sense of something missing and yet on the tip of the tongue.

But of course all this was by way of discovery not strategy. Since he was known through the entire development process as A and embodied by the incomparable Andrew Bennett, we always knew who we were referring to. It certainly never occurred to us that any delicate, momentary unease in having no name to put to a face would be anything more than that. Until the first reviews appeared referring confidently to John or Gerry.

So what do you call someone with no name? Someone could probably clarify all this and show that A is really 'A', but I fear if we go that route we'll end up with Bertrand Russell telling us the set of all anonymous characters should itself remain anonymous and that the king of France is bald.

But back on planet earth it's probably enough to say that so many people worked so hard to make this production possible that it would be impossible to thank them all, even with all the letters of the alphabet. In addition to all the technical support and expertise that fleshed out the naked geometry, there is the generosity of funding bodies and audiences that invite us to keep trying to tell stories.

I am as ever indebted to the good humour and guts of the cast during all stages of this play's development and for making it come alive. It's a pleasure to acknowledge their contribution here – Andrew Bennett, Damian Kearney, Louis Lovett, Ruth McGill and Janet Moran – who all agreed to perform it before a scene was written and in one or two cases before a scene was finished. Thanks also to Tom French for an unwitting line which unlocked the play; to Christian Schiaretti and Clara Simpson, who provided refuge for the initial writing of this project; to Florence et Didier in Villemus, Eoin West and Etáin O'Malley; to Anne Bogart and SITI company for introducing me to the work of Dr Jill Bolte Taylor; to Loughlin Deegan and the International Dublin Theatre Festival, and to the Arts Council of Ireland/An Chomhairle Ealaíon. Lastly I have to thank Sarah Durcan, our producer, unstinting support and champion, and Annie Ryan who is beyond compare.

Michael West
Dublin, June 2010

Characters

A
B
C
D
G

A bare stage.

Spanning the entire width, there are curtains on a rail that can be drawn open and shut.

A screen on which film can be projected.

Two hospital beds on castors which can double as tables.

On either side of the playing space there are wigs and various props. (In the script, real objects are marked in CAPS; all other objects are mimed.) There are also a couple of microphones, which the performers use for the phone calls and all sound effects. There are some chairs and a sofa. These wings are clearly visible to the audience at all times.

*There is a portable camera which becomes **A**'s point of view in the hospital scenes, with the carers looking into it when they talk to him. In these scenes the actor playing **A** stands or sits to one side, watching himself, as it were. As the play begins, the camera is placed downstage centre.*

Episode One

1.1

The company arranges the space for the performance. This includes drawing the curtains and setting one of the beds as a table bearing the leftovers of a party – some Indian TAKEAWAY TRAYS, wine-stained GLASSES and a couple of empty BOTTLES.

*An image comes to life on the screen. It is a close-up of **A**, in pyjamas, sitting in his kitchen talking to **Jack**, his eighteen-year-old son. In the sequence that follows **Jack** is off-screen, holding the camera.*

Film footage – Thursday morning

A   Well ok, but I'm not really going to say anything, because I've nothing to say.

J (*off-screen*)   Can you tell me a little bit about yourself.

A   You know everything.

J (*off-screen*)   I don't. Let's just start somewhere. Where are you from?

A   Limerick.

J (*off-screen*)   Ok, let's do that again. Where are you from?

A   Limerick.

J (*off-screen*)   But you were brought up in Cork.

A   I'm from Limerick.

J (*off-screen*)   And . . .?

A   And I've had a completely normal life.

J (*off-screen*)   In what way?

A   I've done all the normal things, I've been very lucky.

J (*off-screen*)   And is that normal? To think you're lucky. How are you normal?

A   I am normal. I went to school, got an education, I got a job, I got married. I had a son. Who should be in school.

J (*off-screen*)   And you should be at work.

A   Maybe that's how I'm lucky. (*Pause.*) I am lucky. I married your mother.

1.2

Kitchen – Friday morning

*The curtains open revealing **A** in pyjamas sitting at the table.*
***B** is dressed for work and has a dire hangover. She drinks a MUG of tea and watches him.*

B   Are you ok?

A   I've a headache.

B *places the MUG of tea beside him. He doesn't touch it but his heart with his left hand.*

A   I feel . . .

B   I know. I do too. I'm sorry. I'm sorry. But I have to go.

She pulls herself together.

B   I have to go to work. I'll call you later. What are we going to do about Jack?

A   Jack?

B   Will we tell him later?

A   What?

B   Jack. I want to tell him later. About us.

A   Ok.

B   What are *you* going to do?

A   With what?

B   With your life.

Exit **B**.

A   I'm going to . . . I'm going to put out the bins. And bottles.

He goes to clear the table of last night's remains and discovers his right arm isn't quite right. He drops a BOTTLE. He can't tear off a BIN LINER; he struggles to open it. He tidies away the FOIL TRAYS. He has a headache and needs a rest. He gets up and tries to walk and finds he is dragging his right leg.

A   There's something wrong with me. It must be my heart. It's breaking. I need to see a doctor. A doctor. I need help. I'm having a heart attack. It can't be. I had a check-up. Only last month.

1.3

Check up – Last month

A GP's consulting room. **A** *is suddenly able-bodied again.*

D   Is it your leg?

A   No, no. That's an old . . .

D *reads a FILE.*

D   It's a while since your last check up.

A   The fact is, Doctor, I don't know if there really is something wrong with me.

D   Well let's have a look, shall we? Sit up there for me.

D *makes a note.*

A   The fact is for some time now I feel as if there's something missing, something *I'm* missing, you know? I seem to be normal, but I'm not, I feel numb.

D   Where? In the hands or the face?

A   In . . . Inside.

D   Hmmm. Any history of heart attacks, sclerosis, angina, cirrhosis?

A   No.

D   Deformity, insanity, congenital abnormality?

A   No.

D   Syphilis, gonorrhoea, chlamydia, gout?

A   A little indigestion, maybe.

D   Impetigo, scabies, psoriasis, acting rashly?

A   No.

D   Depression?

Pause.

D   A history of depression in your family?

A   Well, my wife . . .

D   *Your* family.

A   O. Well I don't really . . . they're all gone. My mother, my sister.

D   Father?

A   My father died.

D   Aha. Of what?

A   Old age. Eighty something. I hadn't seen him since I was a child.

D   Maybe so, but what killed him?

A   A fall. I think.

D (*makes a note*)   History of falling.

A   Yes! I have the urge to fall down before women I don't know, women I pass on the streets. I want to fall down before them and kiss their knees, I want to hold them, hold them, hold them for the longest time. I see women and wonder when they were last held like that, if they've been loved and adored.

D   I see.

D *examines him. He unscrews a flap in the back of* **A**'*s head and peers inside.*

A   I find myself in tears, I weep doing the simplest things, putting coins in a meter, looking for my keys, making a list. I weep over things I've lost, that I'll never do, over the enormity of things, their insignificance, or because I can't find them. I worry about my son, if he'll ever be happy, if he'll ever find January –

D   Sorry.

D *has inadvertently switched channels by poking his brain.*

A   February, March, April, May –

D *tries to get him back on track and pokes again.*

A   Spoons, spittoons, pots, pans, kettles, kitchen condiments –

D   Just a second.

D *gets him back to normal with a final poke and replaces the screws. While* **A** *talks,* **D** *clambers under the table like a car mechanic, and from beneath drills a bore hole to see what's wrong with* **A**'s *insides. Splinters fly, flies buzz.* **D** *shines a torch up there to make sure he hasn't missed anything.*

A   An indescribable longing, an intense longing, and a reduced capacity to do anything about it. I feel powerless and impotent, unable to respond to my appetites or desires. I feel somehow diminished, that I am less myself. A sense of being off-balance, of blindness, inward-looking pain and discomfort, an inability to recall significant events and thoughts and emotions, a general numbness and insensitivity to life.

D *finishes up his inspection, replaces everything as it was and emerges.*

D   Well nothing too serious. Nothing I could find anyway.

A   Nothing?

D   That's good, isn't it? Look, you probably have too much time on your hands. What you need is a nice long walk, a proper steak, a bottle of wine. And a good laugh.

He leaves, taking the MUG with him.

1.4

House – Friday morning

A *finds himself back in his hall.*

A   How long have I been standing here? The light is different. I can't remember what I'm doing. I'm in the hall. I'm looking for the phone. I'm sinking, turning, falling.

He falls to the floor. His image appears on the screen.

A   I'm looking at the . . . ceiling. I hear a strange hissing, like a leaking tyre or cylinder of gas. It's my breathing. I want to sleep.

The phone rings. The answering machine kicks in.

B (*voice coming over speakers*)   Hi. It's me. It's lunch, after lunch. I tried earlier but couldn't get through. Are you there? I'll wait a sec in case you're going to pick up. Are you going to pick up? You might be out. Anyway. I'm just . . . seeing how you are. And . . . You're not going to pick up. Ok. Bye.

She hangs up.

A   A sound, a rhythmic sound floods through me, apple apple apple apple, it is my blood, my life. I watch the shadow slowly climb the wall and part of me goes with it. I could be lying here for hours or days. I'm coming apart.

The doorbell rings during the above. The phone rings again.

G (*over speaker*)   Hello. It's dry rot. The fungal expert. There's no answer. I'll try one more time.

The doorbell rings repeatedly.

A   I'm here. I'm here.

Thumping on the door.

A   I'm here.

1.5

Rescue

*Two paramedics (**D** and **G**) break down the door and find him on the floor. They lift him on a gurney.*

A   . . . Apple apple apple apple. Thank you. Thank you.

A & E department – Friday afternoon

*A is wheeled in from the ambulance by the paramedics. The arrival comes as a violent shock. Two nurses (**B** and **C**) meet them and begin the triage assessment. It all happens very fast.*

D   You know what's nice with that? An egg.

C   Conscious?

G   In and out.

A   Ah! It's too bright. And loud.

B   What's he presenting?

D   Patient was found collapsed in his own home.

A   What's happening to me?

C   Heart attack?

G   No.

D   Suspected stroke.

C   Stroke.

B   A stroke?

A   What? I can't have a stroke. I have things to do. Dishes, bottles. I have to find Jack. I have to talk to him. I need a phone. Somebody get me a phone.

G   He needs a scan.

C   There's a backlog.

B   What's his blood pressure?

A   Can't you hear me? Why can't you hear me?

G   About 200 over 100.

D   You'd need to check that.

B   Will I check it?

C   Put down 200 over 100.

A   I need to talk to someone. I need to see someone.

G   I need to get a coffee.

D   I need my wheels. Where will we bring him?

B   O god. Not in there.

C   Put him here for the moment.

D   Yeah, but do you have a spare gurney, or . . .?

A *gets up from the trolley bed and watches them leave, unseen and invisible.*

A   Don't go. Don't leave me. I need help. I need to talk to my wife. I need to tell her . . . to ask her . . . Hello? Hello?

1.6

Hospital – Friday evening

Behind a curtain – and looking into a camera mounted on the bed so that their faces loom large on the screen – the doctors and interns hover busily, inserting an IV and taking his pulse, blood pressure and temperature. **A** *watches from the sidelines.*

B   Don't worry, you're going to be fine.

C   Now then, we're just going to take your blood pressure.

D   Hello? Can you hear me? How are you doing today? (*To* **C**.) Blood pressure? I can't read this. What have you got?

C   Blood pressure . . . 200 systolic, over . . .

She releases the cuff and listens with a stethoscope to his brachial pulse.

D (*reading*)   No trauma, medical event, vital signs stable.

B   We checked for hypoglycemia, but his blood sugar's fine.

D (*to* **A**)   Can you squeeze my hand? Ok, can you lift your hand? And this one? (*To* **B**.) Severe motor impairment to the right side.

B   A stroke.

D   An insult to the brain certainly. (*To* **A**.) Don't worry, you're in the right place.

C   106 diastolic.

C has finished taking his blood pressure.

D   Not a heart attack anyway. (*To* **A**.) You've very high blood pressure, we need to do something about that.

C   We have thrombolitics on standby.

D   No blood-thinning agents until we know if he's ischemic or haemorrhagic. Has he had a CAT scan?

B   He's down for one. They're busy.

D   We're all busy. It's Friday. People, we need to see the inside of his head.

B   I'll check about the scan.

Exit **B**.

D   Thank you. (*To* **A**.) We need to take a picture of your brain to see if your stroke is due to a clot or a small bleed. Very important that we know the difference. Then we can work out how to help you. Now let's have a look at your pupils.

D shines a light in his eyes.

A   You're hurting me . . . Ah!

D   What was that?

C   Sorry, that was me.

She's been inserting an IV into his arm. She checks the patient notes.

D   Pupils equally round and reactive to light. (*To* **A**.) We'll find out what's going on in there, ok?

C   There's no name here, and no next of kin.

D   Nothing?

C   No.

D   Nobody knows he's here.

Enter **G**.

G   Lads. You're needed. Two stabbings. One with a screwdriver.

C   He's married, he has a ring.

D   See if someone can find his wife.

Episode Two

2.1

House – Thursday afternoon

A *is on the phone.*

A   I need to speak to my wife. – This is . . . her husband. – Yes, I'd like to leave a message for my wife, Louise. – Well, she uses both names. – No, it's the same person, she just . . . Is my wife there? I think I can hear her. – Look the message is Denis is coming tonight. – Just tell her. She'll know what it means.

Doorbell.

A   Who's this? (*To phone*.) Hello, love. – What I said. Denis is coming tonight. I forgot to tell you earlier. – He said tomorrow didn't suit. – Hang on a second, there's someone at the door.

A *opens the door to find* **G** *as the* **Fungal Man**, *in overalls.*

G   Dry rot?

A   I'm sorry?

G   I'm here about the dry rot. The fungal expert? You arranged an appointment.

Still talking to his wife, **A** *tries to tell the* **Fungal Man** *he's almost done.*

A   Did I? Yes. Come in. (*Back on phone.*) Well he's coming. I've already said yes. And he's bringing his new girlfriend. – I did already. – And I hoovered. – I did that too. – I did them separately. – Don't worry, I'm cooking, everything's sorted. And could you get milk. I forgot. Hello? (*She's hung up. To* **Fungal Man**.) Sorry. My wife.

2.2

Fungal cave – Thursday

A *and* **G** *enter the garage where he shines a torch up at the ceiling.*

G   Technically it's a slime mould, but that doesn't begin to describe its genius. It's a completely different order of life to almost anything on the planet.

A   Dry rot is?

G   *Serpula lacrymans*, yeah. See that? The trails, tendrils? Beautiful stuff. It sends out tendrils through concrete, plaster, wood, actually *through* it, looking for moisture. And when it gets it . . .

He graphically sucks up water.

A   And is it serious?

G   It means business, I can tell you that. How long has it been like this?

A   I don't know. We haven't . . . It hasn't been a problem before.

G   You should have called me a long time ago. People always leave these things until it's too late.

A   Can't we just stick some paint on it? Some anti-mould stuff and cover it up.

G   No, look. You see that?

A   The brown folds there?

G   That's a lovely specimen of fruiting *Serpula lacrymans*. Fruiting. Releasing *millions* of spores. And once it fruits . . . Once it fruits. Do you know a good plumber?

A   I do a bit of . . .

G   Don't get the guy who did this. Or that. You know what this means?

A   No.

G   You are sitting on a time bomb . . .

B (*off*)   Hello? I'm home.

2.3

Hall – Thursday evening

B *enters after a long day at work.*

B   When are they coming? Jack!

A   Eight.

B   I can't believe you asked Denis. I just want to go to bed. Jack!

A   Have a shower. They come, we eat, they go. It'll be fine.

B   We need to talk.

She goes into bedroom to change.

A   We do. I had a man over to look under the stairs and he said we've a pretty serious problem. He says it's been there for years, and we haven't done anything about it.

B   I know.

A   How do you know?

B   He's our son.

A   I'm talking about the dry rot.

B   What?

A   That's what I'm telling you. We have a dry rot infestation and it's threatening the whole house.

B   I don't care about the house. I'm talking about Jack. Where is he?

A   Jack is off with Charlie.

B   The school rang me today. He didn't go in again. Did he say anything?

A   I don't remember.

B   You don't remember?

A   He's got his camera gear, so I don't know when we'll see him. Actually, he's doing a video project. I'm in it. It's quite funny, really. He's so . . . He interviewed me and I found myself telling him . . .

B   You don't seem all that bothered that our son is going to drop out of school. What are you going to do about it?

A   What am I going to do about it?

B   Are you just going to do nothing?

A pause.

A   Will I ask them not to come?

B   It's too late.

A   No, look, I'll just call him.

B   We can't, love. They're practically here.

A   I'll cancel. I'll call him and explain.

B   We invited them.

A   He'll understand.

Doorbell.

B   Let's just try to be nice to each other.

A   Yes. Coming!

2.4

Enter **D** *and* **C** *in OVERCOATS as* **Denis** *and* **Lydia**. *They bear several BOTTLES of wine and a box of CHOCOLATES.*

D   We're not late?

A (*off*)   God no.

C   Or early?

A   God no!

A is handed two bottles of wine which he places on a table. **D** *keeps another for himself and heads off to the living room with it, leaving* **C** *alone.*

D   This one's mine. And this is Lydia.

B (*off*)   Hi Denis!

A   She'll be down in a . . .

A returns and takes her box of chocolates.

A   Let me take that.

A receives her coat and hangs it up.

A   Thank you.

C and D sit on the sofa. **A** *joins them*

C   Denis has told me a lot about you.

A   None of it true, I'm sure.

D laughs loudly.

D   O it's all true. Isn't it?

A I wouldn't know.

D He wouldn't know!

C I believe you were terrible messers back in Cork. At least that's what Denis says.

D You don't believe me? Ask him!

C I think I better. Were you? Did you terrorise the place?

A I wouldn't . . .

D But look how things have changed. Look at us now. Both orphans. Both married to bossy women. Luckily my wife is at home with kids. (*To* **Lydia**.) Sorry love. I promised I wouldn't talk about her and how she's bleeding me dry. Don't break up! You can't afford it. But let's not talk about money either or someone will end up killing themselves. Let's have that drink!

Enter **B**.

B Denis. I'm so sorry about your mother.

D Very sad. But for the best.

They embrace warmly. **A** *nods at the bottle* **Denis** *is hoarding.*

A Do you want me to open that?

D No, no. That's for later.

B Hello, Lydia. Nice to meet you.

C Hi. That's a lovely . . . dress, house you have.

B Thank you.

D Yes, I want to open it myself. Do you have a cork . . .

D *exits to look for a corkscrew.*

A Drink! Yes. What's everyone having?

B Yes please.

A We've wine, we've beer. We've Denis's special bottle.

D (*off*) Don't touch that.

A Lydia. White or red?

C I'm not really drinking at the moment.

A White, then.

C Just a small one, thank you.

A Denis?

D (*re-enters*) Who owns that car outside? It's not yours is it?

A No, that's our neighbour.

B It can't fit in their drive.

A Something to drink, Denis?

D I think I'll just start on my one.

A Well we've actually got some nice . . .

B O yes. It's a special occasion, Denis and . . . Lydia.

C It's lovely to finally meet you both.

D Isn't it? I've told her all about you, about us. Now I need to open that lad. Let it breathe.

C Denis told me what happened to you and your sister. That's so sad. I didn't get to meet Milly, unfortunately, but she sounds like a very kind aunt, person. You were so lucky in a way. I mean, you weren't lucky. You were . . . I just meant you must miss her too. I'm sure you do.

D and **B** *exit silently.*

C I'll just stop talking, will I?

A I'll go and get us all a drink. Something special for the guests . . .

2.5

Fungal cave

A *heads off down a corridor with several turns and stairs that lead into the cramped, dry rot-infested basement. He looks with fascinated horror at the place.*

A   *Serp. Serpula . . .*

Out of the gloom appears the **Fungal Man**.

G   *Lacrymans*. The weeping snakes. That's their name in Latin.

A   Are you still here?

G   All this will have to go. As well as the wet and dry rot . . .

A   The *Serpula* . . .

G   *Lacrymans*, yes, you've damp, mould, and quite a nice fungal infestation behind the radiators.

A   But you can fix it, right? Everything's going to be ok?

G   Well, we can try. But there's something I should . . .

A sees something in the wall.

A   What's that?

G   That? Yeah, I found that earlier. You might want to have a look at it.

A finds a small door which opens into a magical cave.

A   I had no idea.

G   People don't. And it's just under the surface. Go on.

G ushers him on and slips away. **A** *looks about him.*

Some Christmas tree lights flicker unseen. He finds a present. He checks it's for him and that he's alone and shakes it. He shakes it again and listens to its forlorn cardboard rattle.

A   A jigsaw . . .

He drops it to the floor.

2.6

Cork – 1971

C *and* **G** *embrace. They are* **Milly** *and* **Gus**. *They fall into bed and pull up the covers.* **A** *stands watching them wriggle and giggle under the blanket. He is seven.*

G   Chinese, Japanese, look at *these* Christmas trees.

C   Gussy!

G   Jingle bells, Jingle bells, let's go all the way. O what fun it is to ride, on a big, fat—

They are suddenly aware of being watched.

C   Happy Christmas. Was Santa good to you?

G   Go down and play, would you?

A   Well that's what I was thinking, that Santa mightn't actually know I'm here.

C   O?

A   Yes, he might think I'm still living with my Dada and have left my presents there.

C   And who gave you your presents?

A   The jigsaw? Well, I don't know.

C   And the annual.

A   Yeah, the annual. But Denis got an Action Man and toys and stuff, and I was thinking Santa probably left me my real presents in my old house because he didn't know I'd be here, and the jigsaw is probably from my Dada, because he knows I don't like jigsaws. So I was just wondering if we could call him and see if my presents are there. Can we phone him?

C   We'll ring him later, pet.

A   We can't ring him now?

C   Later.

G   It's, what? Seven in the morning! On Christmas!

A   Maybe he'll bring them round.

C   Maybe.

A   Ok. Thanks, Auntie Milly.

C   Now go down and play.

Gus *thinks they're back on.* **A** *doesn't move.*

C   What is it?

A   I was thinking the same thing maybe happened to my sister. Because if I don't know where she is, Santa mightn't either, so that's probably why our toys are back at our home. She's not coming, is she?

C   No.

G   Close the door.

A *leaves. The mood is ruined.* **Milly** *stares after him.* **Gus** *looks at the ceiling.*

A *listens from the hall.*

G   Will he stop asking about her.

C   He *has* stopped asking about her.

G   Isn't he lucky enough that we took him in in the first place?

C   He *has* stopped asking about her.

G   And how long are we supposed to have him?

C   For a while. Until he's settled.

G   He's settled, hasn't he? It's weeks now. He'd be better off with his sister, if he keeps asking for her.

C   He's stopped asking, I told you. Anyhow, they wouldn't be sent to the same place, so they wouldn't be together anyway. And besides I promised Eileen.

G   *I* didn't make any promise.

C   *I* did and I already broke half of it, so I'm not breaking the other half.

G   You were the one who didn't want another baby.

C   I promised my sister.

G It's better that she has a clean start somewhere.

C We should have taken the little baby.

G She'll have more chance of finding somewhere on her own.

C I hope so, Gussy. But he's staying.

G If he puts one foot out of line, one foot.

C We're keeping him.

Denis, *aged eight, approaches* **A** *and stands defiantly before him. He holds out an* ACTION MAN *before going into a spectacular battle sequence with sound effects from which* **A** *is pointedly excluded.*

D (*at imaginary enemy*)   Hand in hoch, hand in hoch!

A *tries to join in, sound effects and all.* **D** *looks on witheringly and repeats his attempts back to him.*

D Pachew, pachew? Spa.

C (*off*)   I heard that, Denis Looby.

Milly *comes by and makes* **D** *give the Action Man to* **A**.

C Give it to him.

D *complies with ill grace. It won't be for long.*

2.7

Caravan, Cork – 1974

*In a cramped caravan with steamed up windows, waiting for the rain to ease. The kids (***A***, ***D*** and ***B***) are playing Monopoly with* **Milly**.

Enter **Gus** *from the tiny bog.*

G I wouldn't go in there for a while, if I was you.

He watches them play for a bit.

G Buy. Why don't you buy?

B I don't have enough money.

G   Borrow it. Who's the bank?

C   We've run out.

G   Write it down.

A   And we've no houses, or only five or something, and he's taken them.

G   Good lad.

B   I wish we were back in America.

G   Denise, we had to come home and help the people in Cork.

C   But for our holidays? O Gussy, why are we here in Courtmac when we could be anywhere where there's sun.

B   Somewhere warm.

C   Can we please go to a country that has weather and not only feckin rain?

G   And how are we going to afford a plane for *five* of us, Milly?

C   Don't start with your budgeting talk, you'll have me up the mouldy caravan wall.

G   Yea, well, money doesn't grow on . . .

C   Didn't you get the new car?

G   That's part of my work! I *have* to drive a Ford, Milly, I *want* to drive a Ford. I work for Ford.

C   You didn't have to buy a stupid yellow . . .

G   Mustard. Mustard.

C   Yellow.

G   Ford is a beautiful company and I am proud to call myself a Ford man.

While their argument continues inaudibly, **Denis** *rubs the window clear of condensation.*

D I can see your father.

A Can you?

D Yes. Look, there he is. He's come to spy on us.

A Where?

D Maybe he's come to take you back.

A I can't see him.

D There. Over there behind the hedge.

A Near the donkey?

D Is that a donkey? I could have sworn . . .

A *looks back at the game in shame.*

D Hee-haw.

Denis *brays, getting louder and louder, as the argument comes back into focus.*

C . . . talking about money, you mean, cold-hearted man. Stop it, Denis. Some things are more important than money.

G That's easy for you to say, since you don't have any.

C Like family. Shut up, Denis.

G This *is* my family.

A I want to go home.

G Well you *can't* go home! We're on holiday now, so we're going to enjoy it.

They leave.

A *is back in the fungal cave unsure of whether he is alone or not.*

A Hello? Dry Rot Man? Anybody there? I'm getting a drink. Something special for our guests.

Uncertainly he takes a bottle and returns to the party to find everyone is gone, the table abandoned. He sits on it.

Episode Three

3.1

Hospital – Friday evening

B (*voice over speaker*)   Hi, it's me again. Are you there? Jack? Are you back? It's about five. Anyway, I'm working late and I'm going to have to talk to someone here when I'm done. So I don't know, eat without me or . . . There should be a bit of Indian from last night. I hope you're ok. That's all. Ok, bye.

Sitting on the table, **A** *is carefully wheeled down a corridor by a nurse* (**C**). *She talks to the camera and her face appears on the screen.*

C   Now how's that? Aren't you grand and comfy?

A   I can't move, I can't speak. Am I still alive?

C   Of course you are. There isn't a proper room ready for you just yet, now is that all right? So we're just taking you down here to a quiet place so you can get some rest, ok?

A   My head, my head is throbbing. The lights are too bright. Breathing hurts my ribs. All I can hear is the blood pumping through my veins, apple apple apple apple, the pressure in my head.

C   Good man. Now here we are. It's only temporary, nothing lasts forever.

She gently tucks him in.

A   Don't leave me. I'm afraid. Talk some more. Tell me I'm going to be all right. Am I always going to feel like this? . . . Are you still there? Is anybody there?

The nurse slips away, pulling the curtain to reveal . . .

3.2

Schoolyard, Cork – 1976

D   I have a photo. Anybody want to see a photo?

A thirteen-year-old **Denis** *shows the lads (***A*** and ***G***) a picture, carefully torn from a magazine. They are amazed and drink it in.*

D   And look at that. And see that? That's a wicker chair.

G   Look at her tits.

A *can't take his eyes off her. Through the following he manages to get a hand on one edge of the picture.*

D   'Tits.' Look at the whole thing.

G   Hole thing.

D   You're not appreciating the quality, lads. That's called backlighting. She's backlit. See the aura around her hair?

G   That's like your mother's hair.

D *slaps him expertly.* **D** *unfolds the picture again and* **A** *resumes his quest to hold it.*

D   See that? That is bamboo. That's a rubber plant. That is a house in America.

A (*reading*)   Penthouse.

D   That's right, yeah. And I was in it.

G   No way.

D   Yep. I was in America.

G   Was she there?

D   Who do you think took the photo?

A   Brother Laurence!

The bell clangs loudly and they look around in alarm. **D** *shoves the photo at* **A** *who pockets it.*

D   Don't tear it, don't tear it. Hi, Brother Laurence!

3.3

The classroom

D *and* **C** *set the chairs.* **A** *sits and surreptitiously inspects the photo.* **B** *is doing an impression of the teacher.*

B   In poetry, the line is divided into metrical units
called . . . What are they called?

G *enters as* **Brother Laurence**, *wearing a black SOUTANE and
carrying a CANE. He paces the classroom.*

G   In poetry, the line is divided into metrical units
called . . . What are they called? Feet. Feet. And what's this
one? Well? Well?

He holds up a long finger.

C   A finger, sir.

G   *This*, you ignoramuses, is a dactyl. A finger. The Greek
for finger. And why is it named after a finger? Because it
resembles the joints of a finger. (*He counts off the joints.*)
Long, short, short. Like what? Like Oliver Gogarty. Like
Malachi Mulligan. Like savages. Savages savages savages
savages. Give me your hand, boy.

D *stretches out a hand in fear and braces for the pain.* **Brother
Laurence** *lightly taps the meter on the open palm.*

G   ONE two three, ONE two three, do you feel it? It's a
waltz, boys. Hickory Dickory, Higgledy Piggeldy. You hear
dactyls in the roll call, we are blessed with dactyls in this
class. Anthony Finnegan, Cassidy, Halligan, Christopher
Comerford, Mickeleen Lonigan. Now what's a trochee?
Well?

D   A foot.

G   A foot, is it? What kind of foot? Short, long, long, short?

D   A trochee is a . . . short and a long.

G   No! You fucking savages. A short and a long is an iamb.
What's an iamb? An iamb is a short and a long. Di dum, di
dum, di dum, di dum. And át my báck I álways hear,
Doreen O'Dea begin her tea. I wandered lonely as a cloud,
away alone alas along begob. But a trochee is its opposite, a
long and a short. Like . . . like *trochee*, a little example of
itself. Like, like, give me something else.

D   Finger!

C   Foot.

A   Apple.

G   Apple, good. Apple apple apple apple. Say it.

D (*to* **A**)   Spapple.

The class say apple softly through the following.

G   Trochees in your educational horizons include chicken licken, henny penny, cocky locky, ducky lucky, turkey lurky, foxy loxy and Father Gerard Manly Hopkins. Trochees in this class include Andrew, Colm, Denis Looby, Dermot, eejit, Eamon Carney, Peter Casey, Peter Farrell, Peter Piper Pumpkin Eater, Michael Collins, DeValera, fitter faster bigger longer, langer, bucket—

*He swoops on **A** who is looking at his photo again.*

G   And what is that you have in your sweaty little hand that means you cannot pay attention to our class? What is it? Show me.

A *refuses.*

G   Stand. Give it to me.

A *stands and hands over the folded photo.* **Brother Laurence** *carefully holds it.*

G   And what is this? Who is this?

He slowly picks a corner and unfolds the image.

A   It's . . . my mother.

Hysteria. The bell goes.

G   Everybody out. Not you. Everybody out. Close the door.

The pupils leave. **A** *is absolutely terrified.* **Brother Laurence** *looks at him seriously, still holding the picture.*

G   I'm disappointed in you. Why is that, do you think? You're not like the rest of those savages. But you've stopped

working. You've stopped trying. And if you don't apply
yourself, how else are you going to get out of here? You still
have your whole life ahead of you. You can't always think
about what you've lost, you know. And you may be a bit
young for this, but you're also free of a lot of things that
hold people back. So I want to put you forward for the
Entrance Exhibition. The Scholarship exam for getting into
college.

A   Is that my punishment?

G   Is that your punishment? If you like. But I think you've
probably had enough punishment as it is.

G *hands the picture back to* **A**.

G   Burn that.

G *leaves*.

3.4

House – Thursday

In the kitchen, **A** *smells something burning. From the dining room
we can hear bits of a heated conversation.*

D   Well it's gone.

B   Yeah, but who's paying for it?

D   Louise. I'm sorry, but . . .

B   We are. We all are.

D   It's not that simple.

B   And Jack, and your kids, and all our kids will be paying
for it for the rest of their lives.

C   And how many kids do you have?

B   What?

*A realises he is burning the dinner and closes the door to the hall.
Their voices become muffled. He wafts the air behind him and opens
a window to let out the smoke. He goes into the hall – we can hear*

their voices again – and finds a phonebook and a sheaf of take-away menus which he hurriedly scans. He picks one and locates the phone.

D . . . Look, we are where we are. We're all responsible and we're in it together. The sooner we accept it the better.

C Denis is writing a book.

B No way.

D Lydia.

B You're not. Are you? Are you really writing a book?

C He is. I'm helping him order his thoughts and, and chapter headings and some of the concepts. I've a lot of books.

B Is it a self-help book?

D (*together*)   No.

C (*together*)   Yes.

D Sort of.

B What's the title?

D I haven't . . .

C *Good Change, Bad Change*, is the working . . . It's really how to adapt to the global warming of emotional and economic ecosystems.

B *guffaws as* **A** *ducks back into the kitchen and closes the door, shutting out their voices once more.*

A Hello? Yes, I'd like to order . . . Can you hear me? I can't talk any louder. I'd like to order a meal for four. I don't actually care what type of food as long as I can get it immediately. What's quickest? Do you do French, or Italian? You're an Indian! I just need dinner for four . . . No, forty-five minutes is too long. It has to be now. How about if I pick up? I'll pick up. Great, I'll pick up. Thank you.

A *hangs up and goes to join them.*

D   It's a shock, I agree with you. It's been profoundly disturbing – but for the best!

B   How can you say that, when people are losing their livelihoods, their . . .

D   Change is always disturbing, but we have to embrace it, because we are changing all the time.

C   Everything is changing.

D   As Lydia says. And that's the point of my book. You'll have to read it. I'll give you one.

They notice him standing there.

B   Are we ready?

A   I'm afraid the potatoes are still not done. I don't know why but they're rock hard.

C   We can wait.

B   Please. I have to eat something.

C   Can we help?

A   No, everything is . . . It's just the potatoes.

D   Potatoes! Even the potatoes have turned against us.

Three bags of CRISPS drop onto the table. They open them, reluctantly at first, and tuck in.

A   There, that's just a . . . while we're waiting. I hope everyone likes Indian.

B *chokes on a crisp and coughs violently.*

C   I love Indian!

D (*to* **A**)   Is it going to be spicy?

C   I hope so. Hot food makes me . . . you know.

D   I'm only asking because this is a very expensive bottle of wine and I want to know if I should drink it all first.

A   Are you ok?

D   That's a bad cough. You should have someone look at that.

C (*searching for water*)   O yes, here.

A   If you . . . arms up.

B (*coughing*)   No, I'm fine.

C   Water. I don't have any.

A   Put your arms up.

B   Get off.

B *gets up to leave*.

A (*to* **Denis**)   I thought, arms up.

B *coughs away*. **D** *raises his arms*.

D   Hand in hoch! Don't shoot. It's a stick up. Give her the Heimlich!

B   Excuse me.

D   Some air. This woman needs air. Clear this lady's passage.

B   Stop!

Exit **B**, *still coughing and laughing, accompanied by* **D**.

C   He's funny, isn't he?

A   Gas.

C   I just don't know how to talk to him sometimes. You just never know if he's . . . You never know how he's going to react. He's so angry most of the time, with his wife, with his work, and he's going away and for how long, and is he, I mean is he, this is a weird thing to ask, but do you think he's changed? I know he's had lots of women, *lots* of women, but do you think he'll . . .?

A   I have to check something.

He tries to slip away but she follows him.

C   Of course you don't know, do you? How can you answer that? I mean, how did you and Louise know you were meant for each other? Was it love at first sight?

3.5

Dorm room, Dublin – 1986

Night. **A** *is studying at his desk.*

A   Gross Domestic Product or Yd equals Consumption plus Investment plus Government spending plus Exports minus Imports. Yd equals $C + I + G + N$. GDP equals GNP minus the net inflow of labour and property incomes from abroad.

Denis (*twenty-three*) *arrives in full flight, carrying two BOTTLES of wine.*

A   Denis?

D   Is Gerry in?

A   No. What are you . . .? What time is it?

D   Time for you to meet some friends.

A   No, no, I'm studying. I have exams tomorrow.

D *talks to some unseen girls.*

D   Come on in girls. Louise. Ciara.

A   I'm sorry, but you can't stay.

D   Of course we're not staying.

A   I have to study.

D   Study us! We're fascinating. Aren't we, girls?

A   I have my finals tomorrow. Tomorrow morning and I can't—

D   It's an amazing threshold. We stand on the threshold of the rest of your life. This is Ciara. Louise.

C   Clara.

D   Who's having what? Who's having who?

*He presents two young girls, **B** and **C** (aged seventeen), and they troop past **A** into his tiny room.*

C   Come on, Louise.

A   You have to go, take them somewhere else.

D   The fact is . . . (*whispers*) I can't bring them anywhere else.

A   Why? Are they . . . No, Denis. You can't. (*To girls.*) Are you two still in school?

D   Now, glasses. Ciara, *Clara*, you follow me.

C *follows* **D** *off into the adjoining room.* **A** *and* **B** *are left alone.*

B   Hi. I'm Louise.

A   Do you know him?

B   No.

A   You can't stay.

From the other room, **D** *uncorks a bottle with a cheer.*

Half an hour later. **A** *and* **B** *sit silently while* **C** *and* **D** *have audible sex next door. Long pause.*

A   Do you like school?

B   Can we please open that bottle of wine?

A *and* **B** *an hour later.*

B *pukes and pukes.*

A   Are you ok? You'll be ok.

B   Sh. I'm ok now. I feel better now. I'm sorry about your books.

A   Would you like a drink?

She certainly does not.

A   Of water. Have some water. Sip it.

B   I feel better. Do you want to kiss me?

A   You should drink something.

B   Kiss me.

A   I'm not sure that you're . . .

B   Don't you want to?

A   It's not that I want or don't want.

B   Come here.

A   You should sit down for a second. Have a rest.

B   Yeah. Sit here with me. Don't go.

D *and* **C** *begin making noise again.*

A   I'm not going anywhere. Denis is. Denis! You've got to go. I have to study. Denis, that's enough. You've got to take these girls home. Their parents will be . . .

B   Can I stay?

A   No.

B   Hold me.

A   Ok. How's that?

B   I've got the spins. You're nice.

A   So are you.

B   No. I'm a very bad girl.

A   No, you just had a bit too much . . .

B   No, I'm a very bad girl. Why don't you kiss me? Is it the . . . Does my breath smell?

She lays a hand in his crotch.

A   What are you doing?

B   Saying thank you. For saving me.

A   I don't think . . .

She starts grappling with his flies and dips her head in his lap.

A   No, no, no. O my god.

She abruptly comes upright.

B   I've got the spins again. Spins.

A   Are you ok?

She steadies herself and then heroically returns to work.

A   Stop, stop, stop. Please.

He fights her off. She struggles onto the bed.

B   I'm just going to . . . lie down for a minute. Ring my mum. Actually, she's not even my mum. I'm adopted.

And she passes out. He watches her sleep and gently tucks her in. He chastely lies down beside her.

3.6

Dublin – 1998

Grey, post-coital moment. He sighs.

A   Thank you, love.

B   That was the worst sex I have ever had, anywhere, at any time. Including college. Including you.

A   I'm sorry. I . . .

B   I just mean that it was *disappointing*.

A   Sorry.

B   Not you. Not only you. I mean me. I should be at my sexual peak. It's all right for you, you're well past yours, but I don't want to give up yet, I want to *feel*. I want an earthquake.

A   I'll try harder, I promise.

B   It's not about that. You and me, we could try all night, all year, all our lives, and I'd never get there.

A   Well, not *never*, just not that last time.

B   O look, it works, it doesn't work. There's not much difference any more. You must feel that too.

A   No. I'm always . . . grateful.

Pause.

B   You're welcome.

A   But I am.

B   I know. But that's not . . . drive. It's not . . . raw.

A   Do you want me to shout a bit?

B   God no.

A   Or say things?

B   No, forget it.

A   I'll do anything. I'll do sexy.

B   Love, you couldn't do sexy if your life depended on it.

A   You be sexy then.

B   I'm really not in the mood.

A   Dance for me.

B   I'm getting sad now.

A   But you said you wanted to spice it up.

B   I don't think we can. It's just feels too weird. Is that Jack?

A   We could try.

B   No. It'd be like . . . It's like we've become brother and sister. We don't have a normal sexual relationship, just a slumbering, over-familiar one that sort of sadly strays over into mild incest every month or so. Or longer.

A   I wouldn't mind if it turned out you were my sister.

B   I'm not sure that's . . .

A   I think it would be amazing if after all this time we found each other and took care of each other.

She is looking at him.

A   I only mean that it would be a happy ending of a sort.

B   In what . . . *How?*

He shrugs.

B   I mean, I hope your sister, wherever she is, did ok, is ok . . .

A   Forget it.

B   But wishing that you'd married her. And had a child with her.

A   I said forget it.

B   And not happily married either.

A   Look, leave it. I shouldn't have mentioned it.

B   O my god.

A   Just leave it. I never said it.

B   How long have you been fantasising this? Have you thought that all along?

A gets up and leaves. He goes into the bathroom and looks at his reflection.

3.7

Bathroom, Cork – 1977

*A (aged thirteen), brushing his teeth, mind wandering. The following action is mimed, supported by live sound effects. He lifts off the lid of the laundry basket. And sees them. His brushing slows and stops. He spits into the sink and drops his brush. He bends and carefully retrieves a pair of **Denise**'s knickers. He stares at them, holding them taut between his fingers. He inspects them gently, then delicately sniffs them.*

B (*off*)   Mum! Denis is being a complete prick.

D (*off*)   Like you'd know.

B (*off*)   Prick.

C (*off*)   Denise! Denis. Everyone. Time for Mass.

B (*off*)   He is. Stop it! You prick!

G (*off*)   Watch your mouth. There's no need for language.

B (*off*)   You didn't see him, Dad.

Instinctively **A** *looks around to make sure he is unobserved. He hurriedly stuffs them into his pocket and goes outside.*

In a quiet part of the garden, **A** *checks he is alone. He reaches into his pocket and produces the KNICKERS – now tangible and perfect. He sniffs them and then greedily inhales.*

Enter **Denis**.

D   What you doing?

A *stuffs them back in his pocket.*

A   Nothing.

D   What's in your pocket?

A   Nothing.

D   I saw you.

A   Just a hanky. I've a cold.

D   Show me.

A   Fuck off, Denis.

D   Show me, or I'll tell. Mum!

He shows **Denis** *the knickers, holding them limply before him.*

D   Put them on. Put them on.

A *gives a tiny shake of his head.*

Denis *makes to tell.* **A** *gives in and bends and tucks up a leg.*

D   No, not like that. On your head.

A *puts the knickers on his head.* **D** *is pleased.*

D   Spa.

Episode Four

4.1

Hospital – Friday night

A is alone again in a corridor.

Medical personnel pass by and ignore him. The sound of their movements is amplified.

B (*voice over speaker*)   Hello, are you there? Hello? I know you haven't called. And I've no way of reaching you if you don't pick up. Are you going to answer? Where are you?

Cars pass and drown out her voice. Other voices are audible.

B   Jack? Jack, are you there? I don't know what to do now. I was going to stay out for a bit, but I wanted to know if you'd heard from Jack.

A woman's voice can be heard asking if she wants another drink.

B (*away from phone*)   In a minute. Actually, no. (*Intimate.*) Maybe you're in bed. I'm just going to come home then. (*Away from phone.*) No, I'm not staying, I have to—

She hangs up.

4.2

Hall door – Thursday

A burst of laughter from **B**, **C** *and* **D**, *off.* **A** *enters, still wearing the knickers, followed by* **Denis**, *laughing.*

D   Relax, come on. We're just having a laugh. I'm sorry. I couldn't help it.

This sets him off again.

A   I have to get the food.

D   I'm coming too. Leave them. They want to talk about us anyway.

A   You don't have to . . .

D   But I do, I do. Let me buy the dinner.

A   No, no, you can't.

D   Nah-ah. I insist.

A   You're our guests, we invited you. You can't be buying us . . .

D   Why not?

A   Because I burned the food!

D   Hey, hey! It doesn't matter. None of it matters. All these attachments, they mean nothing.

A   What?

D   I'm telling you, you have to let go of everything – the past, the future. Because we're all going to die.

A   The food will be getting cold.

D   It's true. Losing everything, my job, my house, my wife, my family – it's the best thing that ever happened to me.

A   I'm happy for you. Now we should . . .

D   Because you don't have these things anyway, and holding on tightly like I did, like you do . . . I mean, wouldn't you like to walk away, leave all this behind?

A   I'm not quite at that stage yet.

D   She'd probably thank you for it. You'd be doing her a huge favour . . .

A   Denis, you may think it's ok to walk away from your responsibilities . . .

D   I'm just winding you up. You're right. I am walking away. There's nothing to keep me here any more. That's why I'm leaving.

A   Have you told Lydia?

D   What?

A   Have you told Lydia.

D   Ah, Lydia. Lydia's been good for me. Helped me see things. Helped me let go of my attachment to things. That's a nice car. Is it your neighbour's?

A   I, em . . .

D   They just leave it out here? You know what these cost? Look it's not locked. Let's get in.

A   Don't, you'll set off the alarm.

D   Why don't we go? Right now. You and me.

A   Denis, it's not yours, you'll set it off.

D   We'll just borrow it. We'll bring it back. Let's do it. Get in.

A   What?

D   Get in.

A   No.

4.3

Cortina, Cork – 1979

D   Get in the car, get in the car.

A   We'll get caught.

D   I dare you. We're just going to sit in it.

They sit and savour the delights of **Gussy**'s *Cortina.*

D   You know what I'm thinking?

A   Starsky and Hutch?

D   Not in a Cortina. You know what I'm thinking?

A   What?

D   Angela McCarthy.

A   Angela McCarthy, yeah. I love her.

D   Imagine if we turned up at Angela McCarthy's.
Hi Angela, we're just dropping by. You want to hop in?

Denis *is holding the key.*

A   That's not the key.

D   Stick it in.

A   I'm getting out.

D   If I took it on my own, you'd just tell.

Denis *reaches across and inserts the key.*

D   I'm turning it on.

A   Stop it.

D   Push your left foot down on the pedal.

A   No.

D   The clutch, step on the clutch.

A *complies and* **Denis** *turns on the ignition.*

D   Feel the power. Baby! Let's go. Let's go!

A *drives off nervously.*

D   Put it into second. Now third. Watch out, watch out!

A *panics and* **Denis** *laughs delightedly. They drive on.*

D   Sorry, sorry. You looked so . . . You're doing well. Don't
crash!

He laughs again.

A   I don't know where we're going.

D   Just drive.

D *tugs the mirror so he can see his hair.*

D   Angela McCarthy will let you drop the hand.

The excitement drains out of the adventure for **A** *and he turns for home.*

D   Why did you turn there?

A   I'm driving.

D   Go straight here.

A *turns again.*

D   What are you doing?

A   We're going home.

D   Home? Coward.

A   Yes! Yes and we're going home.

D   Well it's hardly your home, is it? Your home is some boggy field with your Da humping sheep, pretending they're your sister.

A   Shut up.

D   Your poor baby sister. Baaaba. Baaabaa.

A   Shut up.

D (*sings*)   Your poor little sheep who's lost her way, baa, baa, baa.

A *brakes sharply.*

A   Get out of the car.

D   What, thirty yards from our house? Sorry, my house.

A   Get out.

D   If you'd driven to Angela McCarthy's then at least you could have dumped me at the side of the road. Like your sister. Like your baabaa –

A *punches* **Denis** *suddenly in the head.* **Denis** *is astonished and then rouses to action.*

D Don't you touch me, you filthy –

A *punches him again. They grapple in the car. And don't see that* **Gus** *has slunk up beside them.*

G The fuck do you think you're doing?

D Hi Dad.

G Get out of the car.

They obey.

C (*off*) Gussy! Did you find them?

D Sorry, Dad.

A Sorry.

D But we weren't going anywhere . . .

G Don't be smart! You've driven it to here, didn't you?

Milly *arrives to cool them down.*

C Gussy, we don't beat them, remember? We shout at them.

G I am shouting. Now, go into the house.

C Be nice to your father, boys. Your daddy's upset.

G I'm not his fucking father.

C They're closing the factory.

D Ford is closing?

G Think they can treat people like that. Welcoming them into the bosom of the family for how many years? And they turn around and drop you. I will not stand for it. I will not stand for it.

Gussy *has a violent turn, trashing the car to the astonishment of the boys. He breaks down in tears.* **Milly** *comforts him.*

G That was my car. I loved that car.

C   Gussy.

G   What am I going to do, Milly? What are we going to do?

C   It's all right, Gussy, we'll manage.

They depart. **Denis** *and* **A** *share a look and* **A** *takes the knickers off his head. Exit* **D**.

4.4

Hospital

A *gets onto his bed and lies down.* **B** *and* **C** *make the rounds. They can barely be heard. Music plays over the scene.*

C   Is he ready for a scan?

B   Are they taking him now?

C   The machine was down earlier. Anyway, they're ready. He hasn't eaten or drunk anything?

B   Doesn't look like it.

C   They want him to have contrast. Will you fit it? The back of the hand.

Enter **D**.

C (*to* **A**)   You have to lie still, otherwise they won't be able to do the scan.

D   Is he ready? I'm to take him down.

C   Bring him down.

They wheel the gurney into the corridor and down to Radiology.

C   Administer a mild sedative through the IV. If he's restless they can clamp him. It's very quick. They just need to keep the head still while they do the scan.

A *is fed into the CAT scanning machine. His image appears on the screen as the lights pass over him.*

*A porter (**G**) then wheels him into the next scene.*

4.5

Dinner party – Thursday

*With **A** still lying in state on the table, the others eat their take-away around – and possibly including – his remains.*

D   Lydia's qualifying as a homeopathist.

Pause.

B   Good for you. I think herbal medicine is really important.

A   It's not herbal medicine.

D   And she cured a baby of . . . what was it, darling?

C   Croup.

D   I was going to say meningitis!

B   Well, who knows? I mean there's things in plants we haven't even begun to understand.

A   Yes, but it's not herbal medicine.

D (*drinking*)   You know, I can't taste this at all.

B   I envy you, actually, helping people, and so naturally.

A   Homeopathy is not herbal medicine.

B   Isn't it?

A   No, it's nothing.

C   No.

A   Sorry. Tinctures of nothing.

B   I can't believe you just said that.

A   Sorry.

D   You can't just dismiss alternative healing practices like that. (*To **Lydia**.*) Can he?

B   What do you know about herbal medicine anyway?

A   Homeopathy is not herbal medicine.

B   It is.

A   I'm just pointing out a fact.

B   It's herbal medicine.

A   It isn't. Tell her, please. Is it herbal medicine? Is it herbal medicine?

C   They're extracts.

B   Ha!

A   Reduced to nothing.

C   No.

A   Diluted to nothing.

C   No.

A   They *were* extracts, maybe, before they're diluted a million times, to nothing.

B   They're extracts.

D   Can't taste a thing.

A   Parts per million! Parts per million! Even if there *was* rosemary or thyme or mint in it a hundred years ago there isn't any more. *I* contain more rosemary than those pills.

B   I can only apologise for my husband. Did everyone have enough?

C   It was very nice, thank you.

A   I'm just saying.

B   More wine?

D   No thanks.

C   No.

A   (*to himself*)   Dispersed molecules.

B   Anyone for coffee? Tea?

A   Trace atoms.

B   Coffee, Lydia?

A   That's all.

C   No, thanks. It doesn't agree with me.

D   Neither does Professor Penthouse there.

B   Tea, then? Herbal, maybe?

D   Herbal!

C   Maybe, yes.

B   How about you, Denis?

A   Denis, what do you think of it?

D   Hmm?

B   Tea or coffee?

A   Is this part of the new Denis, the new changed Denis?

D   I don't know, I'm just . . . It's Lydia's . . .

B   Leave him alone. What are you having, Denis?

A   Of course, you're supporting Lydia. I mean, that's right, you should support Lydia.

B   Leave it, please, we're having a conversation.

A   You wouldn't want to leave her twisting in the wind. But she's a right to know what you think, more than any of us, doesn't she, don't you? So I'm only asking . . .

B   Don't answer him. More wine?

A   What do you think, Denis? Is there something to it, or do you think it is complete and utter donkey pizzle?

All turn to **Denis**.

D   The mind . . . is a powerful tool.

Long pause.

B (*claps*)   Well said.

A   Do you mean placebo?

B   Gone. Done. Tea, coffee.

A   Denis. Are you talking about the placebo . . .

B   It's over! Denis, what do you want!

D   I'm trying to make up my mind.

B   Well at least you haven't closed yours off.

D   Why don't I help you?

B   You don't have to do that.

D   I want to.

B   Do you?

D   Watch me. A cup of tea, a cup of gall, and how about . . .

Denis *deliberately spills a drink on* **B**. *She looks at him and then at the spill.*

D   Look what I've done.

B   I'll have to change.

D   Don't change. I love you just the way you are.

She laughs.

D   I do. I love the colour, the cloth, the cut.

B   The cut of it.

D   And look, it's easily cleaned.

He dabs the spill very gently.

D   There's a little bit. And there's a little bit. And there's a little bit. And there's a little bit.

B   I'll have to soak it.

She looks at him and walks away.

D   I'm going to make some coffee.

Denis *leaves* **A** *and* **C** *alone.*

C   My father died of cancer.

He smiles helplessly.

C   It was very unpleasant for him. They couldn't do anything for him. But they gave him chemo anyway. And they killed him. I really believe that. But I don't believe in suffering. Pain is a reality. But suffering is what you allow to happen. To yourself. To others. And for my father, dying, I know that iced water, anything, a walk, a quiet conversation, were better for him than what they did to him. That's all. Do you have a bathroom?

A   Yes. No. Look, I apologise for going on like that, before. I'm sorry. I'm terribly sorry. Would you like anything?

C   I'd like Denis to love me. Because I love him. I love him.

A   The bathroom! The bathroom. The small one is downstairs, but the flush is . . . there's a kind of knack to it. And there's a bigger one . . . Shall I show you?

C   I don't know what to do. I mean, nothing, obviously. He says he loves me and I want to believe him but I just don't, isn't that weird? That I want the man I love to say he loves me and when he does it isn't enough. And now he's going away and I'm worried that he's not coming back and I don't know what to do. Should I follow him or give him an ultimatum or just let him do whatever he wants. Is that what love is?

A   Like I said. Down the hall. Or upstairs. I'm just . . . I need a whiskey.

He steps out and finds himself back in hospital. He lies down on the bed.

Episode Five

5.1

Hospital – Friday, 11p.m.

Enter **B** *escorted by a doctor* (**D**). *She is in shock.*

B   Where is he? What's happened to him?

D   Well he's had some kind of stroke, but we don't yet know how severe the damage is to his brain.

B   He has brain damage.

D   We're waiting for a consultant to confirm the results of the scan, but it seems he has a brain tumour and it's caused a small bleed.

B   Is he ok? Can he talk?

D   Not at the moment.

B   Can he move?

D   His body is in shock and it may recover some or part of its function.

B   Or it may not. That's what you're saying, isn't it?

She sees him lying completely still.

D   It's really too early to say how permanent the damage will prove. The consultant may decide to operate, or he may not. We're just going to have to wait and see how your husband responds. Now, when did you last see him?

B   When? This morning. I went to work.

D   Can I ask you, did he exhibit any symptoms?

B   What?

D   Headaches, nausea, problems with vision.

B   I don't know.

D   Did he complain of numbness or dizziness?

B   No, not that I was aware of.

D   Is there any history of stroke or aneurysm or brain attack in his family?

B   I don't know.

D   Is there any way we could find out?

B   I don't know his family. He doesn't have one. He doesn't have any family.

D   I'll leave you alone with him for a minute.

Exit **D**.

B *looks at him without saying anything.*

Finally she sits by his head and strokes his hair.

5.2

Flashback – 1969

A   Mum. What do you look like when you're dead?

B   You look like you're asleep, dear.

A   I mean in Heaven. What does everybody look like?

B   They look like themselves, dear.

A   Can you recognise everyone? Will Granny look like Granny? Will she be old? And Grandpa, he died when he was young, so will he look young? How do we know?

B   You'll just know.

A   How do we know?

B   It's like wearing a different hat, or something. Or different clothes.

A   I'll know what you look like and you'll recognise me too?

B   Don't worry, you'll always know it's me.

A   How?

B   Because I'll come up to you like this and give you a kiss like this.

He winces.

A   I don't like kisses. Will we have lips?

B   Even if we don't have bodies or shapes –

A   Or hats or clothes.

B   We'll always know each other, and when I come up to you I promise you'll know it's me. Now, go to sleep. Go to sleep or your Dada'll be getting cross. Good night.

A   Good night.

She leaves. In the dark, **A** *whispers . . .*

A   Mum? Mum? Are you there? Mum? Mummy?

5.3

Fungal cave

A gets up and goes down into the cave. The **Fungal Man** *is packing up his stuff.*

A   What are you doing?

G   Finishing up.

A   Don't go. Stay for a drink!

G   Ah, no. I can't.

A   You will.

G   I shouldn't.

A   Do. Stay for a drink. You must.

G   You know, I will.

A   Good. Come up and say hello.

G   Will they mind?

A   No, no. In fact I doubt they even miss me.

G   Am I ok like this? Should I change?

A   No, no. It's casual. Very relaxed. I just came down to get another bottle. It's quite nice in here, isn't it? Very nice, actually. I should have some good whiskey. And some glasses. You know we might just stay here for a bit. There's no rush.

G   It's your house.

A   It is, isn't it?

He goes to find his prize whiskey.

A   How's it all going?

G   Well you'll have to strip everything back to the foundations. The plaster, the insulation, most of that concrete will all have to come out. There's chemical treatment, you can't stay here during that and then it's new stairs, rewiring, replastering. It's going to cost you a lot of money. You are insured, aren't you?

A *runs off and fetches* **Brother Laurence**'s *SOUTANE*.

A   Would you mind terribly changing after all?

G   Sure.

G *gets dressed as* **Brother Laurence**.

G   Do you want me to say anything?

A   No. (*Pause.*) I'd hoped you'd be able to help me. But it's . . . I was looking for something.

G *shuffles off.*

5.4

Nursing home – a few months ago

A *finds a nurse.*

B   And have you been before?

He shakes his head.

B   Well she wouldn't remember it even if you had. She will remember things from far back. But be gentle and calm.

A *turns around and sees* **Milly** (*seventy-six*).

A   Hello, Milly. It's me. You remember me?

Pause.

A   It's nice and . . . cosy. Nice tree.

C   I love Christmas!

A   Yes. I always think of you at Christmas. My first Christmas with you. You're looking well. Are you happy here? Are they . . . Are you happy?

Long pause.

C   I love the smell of pine trees.

A   Me too. Anyway. I wanted to ask you about your sister. Your sister, Eileen.

C   My sister?

A   Yes. Your sister, my mother.

C   My sister is dead. Very sad.

A   That's right.

C   Poor Eileen. So young.

A   That's right. But before she died, she asked you something. What did she ask you?

C   Ask me?

A   When she was young.

C   She asked if I'd . . . be her bridesmaid. She's very pretty. Do you know her?

A   I need to know where my sister is. I've tried. I've looked everywhere and there really are no records. Can you help me, Milly? Do you know anything about my sister?

C   My sister is dead. Very sad.

A   *My* sister. The little baby. Remember the little baby?

C   The baby?

A   Yes, there was a baby. A baby girl. And you gave her up.

C   The baby.

A   You must have heard something. You must know something, Milly. I need you to tell me.

C   I can't.

A   You can.

Milly *is frightened and upset.*

A   You have to think. I need to find her.

C   We wanted to take the baby.

A   Yes, but you didn't.

C   A baby girl.

A   Yes.

C   Where is she?

A   I . . . don't know.

C   We should have taken the little baby. We should have taken the little baby. We should have taken the little baby.

*Another nurse (**D**), comes over and attends to a distraught **Milly**.*

D   Now look what you've done. Milly, calm down. Milly, calm down. Be quiet. There's no baby. No baby. There is no baby. Everything's ok. Look at the tree. See the decorations? Look at the Christmas tree.

She looks up in delight.

C   Nobody told me it was Christmas.

A   Thanks, Milly.

C   Thanks a million.

A   Thanks a million.

C (*to* **D**)   I love the smell of pine.

Episode Six

6.1

Hospital bedside – Saturday

A watches B talking into the camera where his body used to be. His POV is projected onto the screen.

B   Where's that nurse? I can't find him. I've left messages, on his phone, with his friends, but nobody knows where he is. You know what he's like. They're supposed to be taking you for another scan. And there's a consultant, somewhere. I don't know when they're going to see you. It's very hard to see you here like this. I don't know if you can hear me, though that might be a blessing after everything I've said.

A   Just keep talking to me.

B   I've been thinking about you all day. How kind you've been, from the moment I met you. You've been such a good man.

A   No.

B   Such a good husband and father. And I've been a terrible wife.

A   No, no.

B I've become so hard. So dissatisfied. I've always wanted more, I always wanted something else, and it's made me sick, sick to the point I want to throw up my life. And I know it's a ridiculous thing to say in the circumstances, but it doesn't have to be like this any more.

A Hold my hand.

B Because if this is who we are now, if this is our lives, then I want you to know I'm here. I'm here for you.

A Stay with me.

B I'll help you. You don't need to be afraid of anything. Everything will be all right.

A Yes.

B Everything is going to be ok. I don't want you to worry. I don't want you to suffer. You don't have to take care of us all any more. And if you don't want to stay . . . If you want to go, go.

A No, I . . .

B Don't let us hold you back.

A No, I haven't finished.

B Because we'll be fine.

A No, look. I'm still here. I'm still here.

B That's all I wanted to say.

A I'm not ready to go anywhere.

She gets up and makes to leave.

B I'm going to try Jack again.

A Don't go. Listen to me. I need help. Why can't you hear me.

B He won't be able to find . . .

A Look, I can move my toe. Look! I'm moving it.

She has seen the tiniest movement in his foot.

B Did you do that?

A Yes!

B Can you hear me?

A Yes!

B Can you understand me?

A Can you understand me?

B If you can understand me, move your foot.

With great effort he twitches his toe.

B O my god. You're still here . . .

A Yes. I'm going to get better. I'm going to get out of here.

B I have to call someone. Nurse! I need a nurse. Doctor! I'll be right back.

She leaves and starts to hunt down some hospital staff.

B Nurse! Doctor! Help me! I need help! Somebody help him!

A *frantically starts putting out all the remains from the night before on the gurney.*

A We can start over again. Let me show you. We can make a fresh start. Let me show you.

He sets the table the way it was at the top – BOTTLES, TAKEAWAY TINS, GLASSES. The others glide on and assist him.

A Thank you. Thank you.

6.2

Thursday – late

B *slumps into the sofa, laughing wearily at herself.*

B It's like I haven't been here. I've been away and missing my life. I've become so hard, hard and fat. And ugly. I'm so ugly.

A *starts to move towards her but is overtaken by* **Denis**.

A & D   You're not ugly.

B   Ugly. Gross. Disgusting.

D   You're not disgusting.

B   What are you, some kind of compliment machine? Look at me, I'm disgusting.

D   You're not.

Denis *sits beside her on the sofa.* **A** *looks helplessly on.*

B   What am I then?

D   Angry.

B   O yes.

D   Disappointed. Frustrated.

B   What? Don't.

D   Guilty. Sad. Passionate.

B   I know what you're . . .

D   Warm, alive.

B   No I'm not.

He takes her hand.

D   How about here?

She takes it back.

B   No, you.

He takes her forearm.

D   How about here?

She doesn't respond, but neither does she take her arm away. He continues his search for life, touching her gently in her palm, the crook of her elbow, her inner arm, her shoulder, her neck, her nape.

D   How about here? How about here? And here?

B   Maybe a little.

Denis *slowly, slowly moves in for the kill.*

C *is sitting, rather drunk, at the table, telling* **A** *how it is.*

C   The thing is, the thing is, if you love someone, you love them. And there's nothing you can do about it. Is there? Because if you can help yourself, then you're not helplessly, you know, in love. And if it's all . . . control. If it's all . . . deliberate. Then it's not . . . free. Am I right? And if you love someone, you would do anything for them. Anything. That's what it means, am I right? So I've decided. I've decided, I'm letting him go.

D *and* **B** *embrace. He pulls her towards him, but she gets an arm up under his chin to keep him at bay. He keeps wrapping his arms around her as she twists and struggles to escape. They clamber over each other as if they were determined to get past a particularly inventive and resilient octopus. They roll onto the floor.*

A   What are you doing?

B   Me? I'm . . . entertaining.

A   What am I supposed to do?

B   Talk to Lydia. Tell her something.

D *and* **B** *resume their struggle. They are swimming across the floor, past furniture and obstacles, knocking things over, taking things with them as they travel.*

A *begins his story, getting sadder and sadder the further he goes.* **B** *and* **D** *get correspondingly more animated.* **C** *watches impassively.*

A   There was this donkey, an old donkey, and it died on the side of the road, and some lads thought it would be funny to cut off its mickey and use it for a football. So they kick it around in the dust and then they throw it over the wall of the convent, and it lands there where a young nun sees it and picks it up. And the young nun brings it to the Reverend Mother, because she knows everything, and shows it to her and the Reverend Mother looks at it and says, 'Oh no. Father McCarthy.'

He is weeping. **Brother Laurence** *is having a* WHISKEY *in the wings and laughs heartily.*

G   That's a good one.

C   Another drink.

D   Haven't you had enough?

C   No. I want another drink.

B   Give her another drink.

Brother Laurence *moves to the table and pours himself another drink.* **A** *picks up a* BOTTLE.

A   This is dead.

C   Minother drink.

B   Get her another drink.

G   That's a good one, all right.

C   I don't want to be alone. I don't want to be abandoned. I don't want to get old. I don't want to be ugly. I don't want to give up my life.

A   Yes. Life is precious.

A *pokes* **C** *as the music picks up in tempo and volume.*

B *and* **D** *climax.*

A   Get up. We have to dance.

C   I couldn't.

A *hauls her up and whirls her round. She squeals in protest and staggers off.*

C   O no, I'm going to . . . I'm going to throw up.

She throws up off-stage.

A   Is she ok? Is she going to be all right? Is she going to be all right? Is she going to be all right?

6.3

Hospital – 1971

His trauma makes him appear vulnerable and young. Up on the screen, **C** *slowly approaches the young boy as* **Milly**.

C   Would you like to say goodbye to her?

Clearly he doesn't.

C   Will you say goodbye to your mother?

He gives the tiniest shake of his head.

C   You're going to stay with us for a little while, ok? Denis is about your age. You like Denis, don't you? That'll be fun, won't it?

Denis *gets up from lying with* **B** *and walks past him to the sofa.*

6.4

Sitting room

Lydia *re-enters.*

C   I'm sorry, I think I made a bit of a mess in there.

A *gets their COATS.*

C (*to* **D**)   Did I make a show of myself? Will you forgive me? You're not going to leave me are you?

D   Come on. We're going home.

C   You're not going to leave me, are you?

Denis *and* **Lydia** *leave.*

6.5

Thursday night, Friday morning

Dawn is slowly breaking. **B** *lies on the sofa.* **A** *sits at the table.*

B I'm done. Look at me. It's gone. If you want to go, go. (*Pause*.) I want to go. You live here with Jack. You're not going to say anything, are you?

She leaves.

A Do you think we should get a DNA test?

B (*off*) What?

A To be sure.

B (*off*) Don't do this.

A So that we don't have to keep wondering.

B (*off*) No, no, no, no. I'm too tired.

A If there was even the slightest chance that we were . . .

B (*off*) Imagine if . . . I can't believe you'd even *say* that to me.

A Don't you want to know?

B No!

She comes back on.

A You should find out, maybe your family are still . . .

B They're not my family, they're birth parents, they're gone.

A But they mightn't be, you don't know, they might be looking for you.

B They gave me away. They put me up for adoption for a reason.

A They might need to find you, they might have to tell you something.

B That's *my* business. Maybe one day I *will* want to find them, but at the moment I don't, and I certainly don't just to please you.

A   I'm only trying to help you find . . .

B   But you're not trying to help me, you're obsessed with making me somebody else. Why do you persist with this fantasy? Why? How do you think me being your sister would save our marriage?

A   I don't.

B   I'm not your sister! Why do you keep at it? I can't bear it! Why do keep at it?

A   Because it would mean she was loved. It would mean somebody loved her. Not very well, not like she deserved. But somebody loved her. And didn't just leave her. Abandon her. And it would mean I didn't let her down. Didn't let her down.

She regards him for a while and then leaves.

Brother Laurence *tries but fails to say something before he, too, departs.*

Kitchen – Friday morning

B *is dressed for work and has a dire hangover. She drinks a MUG of tea and watches him. He has a headache.*

B   Are you ok?

A   I've a headache.

B *places the mug of tea beside him. He doesn't touch it but his heart with his left hand.*

A   I feel . . .

B   I know. I do too. I'm sorry. I'm sorry. But I have to go.

She pulls herself together.

B   I have to go to work. I'll call you later. What are we going to do about Jack?

A   Jack?

B   Will we tell him later?

A   What?

B   Jack. I want to tell him later. About us.

A   Ok.

B   What are *you* going to do?

A   With what?

B   With your life.

Exit **B**.

A   I'm going to . . . I'm going to put out the bins. And bottles.

He starts to clear the table as he did before and drops a BOTTLE.

The others come on and take over from him. They strike the set. The lights are very bright.

6.6

Final consultation

D   I think we're done.

A   Really?

D   Yes. You're finished.

A   That's it? I'm done?

D   Yes, you just have to leave.

A   O, sorry. Should I thank you?

D   Some people do. Some people are not at all happy. You are one of the quiet ones.

A   Is that good?

D   It makes absolutely no odds.

D *resumes his tidying, with* **B**, **C** *and* **G**.

A   Do I have to sign, or pick up a form, or . . .

D   No, no.

A   It's just I feel like there's something I'm supposed to have done, something I should have . . .

D   Well . . . You should have thought of that earlier.

They're almost done. Music.

A   No, wait, it's important. There are things I haven't said. Things I want to say again. I need to think. I need more time. My son, I haven't seen my boy. I have to see my boy. I have to see my boy. I need to see him one more time. I'm not ready. There's too much I haven't done. It's not time. I don't want to go!

The others step away into the darkness. **A** *softens with pleasure as the lights begin to dim around him.*

B (*over microphone*)   Talk to him. Say something.

J (*voice off*)   Hi Dad. I'm here.

A   Jack! You came. I knew you'd come. Talk to me.

J (*voice off*)   Are you ok?

A   Just keep talking. I want to hear you talking. Even when I can't hear what you're saying.

The light is getting fainter.

A   That light is too bright. Wait, I'll close my eyes, I don't even need to see you, just to hear you, to know you're there. I'm so glad you're here. I'm still here, I'm still, it's still too bright. It's so bright! There's too much noise. It just needs to be quiet. Listen. Apple apple apple apple. Sh, almost. Apple apple almost. Apple, sh. Apple. Ap. Ap. Ap. Free.

The last syllable turns into the continuous beep of a heart monitor as it flatlines.

Blackout.

Film footage – Thursday morning

The screen comes to life with an image of **A** *laughing.*

A   Well I don't know.

J (*off-screen*)   You must know something.

A   I don't, I really don't. That's something you'll have to work out for yourself.

J (*off-screen*)   But your experience must . . . What lessons, what advice would you like to share with me, then?

A   With you? Be nice. Be nice to your mother. (*Pause.*) All this thing about change . . . I think it's hard for people to change. But sometimes it's not about changing at all, it's letting go of trying to be something you're not, I don't know. You, for example. You're perfect the way you are. Is that it? Am I done? Are we done?

He smiles at his son. Fade out.

Lights come up on the empty space.

Methuen Drama Student Editions

Jean Anouilh *Antigone* • John Arden *Serjeant Musgrave's Dance*
Alan Ayckbourn *Confusions* • Aphra Behn *The Rover* • Edward Bond
Lear • *Saved* • Bertolt Brecht *The Caucasian Chalk Circle* • *Fear and
Misery in the Third Reich* • *The Good Person of Szechwan* • *Life of Galileo* •
Mother Courage and her Children • *The Resistible Rise of Arturo Ui* • *The
Threepenny Opera* • Anton Chekhov *The Cherry Orchard* • *The Seagull* •
Three Sisters • *Uncle Vanya* • Caryl Churchill *Serious Money* • *Top Girls*
• Shelagh Delaney *A Taste of Honey* • Euripides *Elektra* • *Medea* •
Dario Fo *Accidental Death of an Anarchist* • Michael Frayn *Copenhagen*
• John Galsworthy *Strife* • Nikolai Gogol *The Government Inspector* •
Robert Holman *Across Oka* • Henrik Ibsen *A Doll's House* • *Ghosts* •
Hedda Gabler • Charlotte Keatley *My Mother Said I Never Should* •
Bernard Kops *Dreams of Anne Frank* • Federico García Lorca *Blood
Wedding* • *Doña Rosita the Spinster* (bilingual edition) • *The House of
Bernarda Alba* • (bilingual edition) • *Yerma* (bilingual edition) • David
Mamet *Glengarry Glen Ross* • *Oleanna* • Patrick Marber *Closer* • John
Marston *Malcontent* • Martin McDonagh *The Lieutenant of Inishmore* •
Joe Orton *Loot* • Luigi Pirandello *Six Characters in Search of an Author*
• Mark Ravenhill *Shopping and F***ing* • Willy Russell *Blood Brothers*
• *Educating Rita* • Sophocles *Antigone* • *Oedipus the King* • Wole
Soyinka *Death and the King's Horseman* • Shelagh Stephenson *The
Memory of Water* • August Strindberg *Miss Julie* • J. M. Synge *The
Playboy of the Western World* • Theatre Workshop *Oh What a Lovely
War* Timberlake Wertenbaker *Our Country's Good* • Arnold Wesker
The Merchant • Oscar Wilde *The Importance of Being Earnest* •
Tennessee Williams *A Streetcar Named Desire* • *The Glass Menagerie*

Methuen Drama Modern Plays

include work by

Edward Albee
Jean Anouilh
John Arden
Margaretta D'Arcy
Peter Barnes
Sebastian Barry
Brendan Behan
Dermot Bolger
Edward Bond
Bertolt Brecht
Howard Brenton
Anthony Burgess
Simon Burke
Jim Cartwright
Caryl Churchill
Complicite
Noël Coward
Lucinda Coxon
Sarah Daniels
Nick Darke
Nick Dear
Shelagh Delaney
David Edgar
David Eldridge
Dario Fo
Michael Frayn
John Godber
Paul Godfrey
David Greig
John Guare
Peter Handke
David Harrower
Jonathan Harvey
Iain Heggie
Declan Hughes
Terry Johnson
Sarah Kane
Charlotte Keatley
Barrie Keeffe

Howard Korder
Robert Lepage
Doug Lucie
Martin McDonagh
John McGrath
Terrence McNally
David Mamet
Patrick Marber
Arthur Miller
Mtwa, Ngema & Simon
Tom Murphy
Phyllis Nagy
Peter Nichols
Sean O'Brien
Joseph O'Connor
Joe Orton
Louise Page
Joe Penhall
Luigi Pirandello
Stephen Poliakoff
Franca Rame
Mark Ravenhill
Philip Ridley
Reginald Rose
Willy Russell
Jean-Paul Sartre
Sam Shepard
Wole Soyinka
Simon Stephens
Shelagh Stephenson
Peter Straughan
C. P. Taylor
Theatre Workshop
Sue Townsend
Judy Upton
Timberlake Wertenbaker
Roy Williams
Snoo Wilson
Victoria Wood

Methuen Drama Modern Classics

Jean Anouilh *Antigone* • Brendan Behan *The Hostage* • Robert Bolt *A Man for All Seasons* • Edward Bond *Saved* • Bertolt Brecht *The Caucasian Chalk Circle* • *Fear and Misery in the Third Reich* • *The Good Person of Szechwan* • *Life of Galileo* • *The Messingkauf Dialogues* • *Mother Courage and Her Children* • *Mr Puntila and His Man Matti* • *The Resistible Rise of Arturo Ui* • *Rise and Fall of the City of Mahagonny* • *The Threepenny Opera* • Jim Cartwright *Road* • *Two & Bed* • Caryl Churchill *Serious Money* • *Top Girls* • Noël Coward *Blithe Spirit* • *Hay Fever* • *Present Laughter* • *Private Lives* • *The Vortex* • Shelagh Delaney *A Taste of Honey* • Dario Fo *Accidental Death of an Anarchist* • Michael Frayn *Copenhagen* • Lorraine Hansberry *A Raisin in the Sun* • Jonathan Harvey *Beautiful Thing* • David Mamet *Glengarry Glen Ross* • *Oleanna* • *Speed-the-Plow* • Patrick Marber *Closer* • *Dealer's Choice* • Arthur Miller *Broken Glass* • Percy Mtwa, Mbongeni Ngema, Barney Simon *Woza Albert!* • Joe Orton *Entertaining Mr Sloane* • *Loot* • *What the Butler Saw* • Mark Ravenhill *Shopping and F***ing* • Willy Russell *Blood Brothers* • *Educating Rita* • *Stags and Hens* • *Our Day Out* • Jean-Paul Sartre *Crime Passionnel* • Wole Soyinka • *Death and the King's Horseman* • Theatre Workshop *Oh, What a Lovely War* • Frank Wedekind • *Spring Awakening* • Timberlake Wertenbaker *Our Country's Good*

Methuen Drama Contemporary Dramatists

include

John Arden (two volumes)
Arden & D'Arcy
Peter Barnes (three volumes)
Sebastian Barry
Dermot Bolger
Edward Bond (eight volumes)
Howard Brenton
  (two volumes)
Richard Cameron
Jim Cartwright
Caryl Churchill (two volumes)
Sarah Daniels (two volumes)
Nick Darke
David Edgar (three volumes)
David Eldridge
Ben Elton
Dario Fo (two volumes)
Michael Frayn (three volumes)
David Greig
John Godber (four volumes)
Paul Godfrey
John Guare
Lee Hall (two volumes)
Peter Handke
Jonathan Harvey
  (two volumes)
Declan Hughes
Terry Johnson (three volumes)
Sarah Kane
Barrie Keeffe
Bernard-Marie Koltès
  (two volumes)
Franz Xaver Kroetz
David Lan
Bryony Lavery
Deborah Levy
Doug Lucie

David Mamet (four volumes)
Martin McDonagh
Duncan McLean
Anthony Minghella
  (two volumes)
Tom Murphy (six volumes)
Phyllis Nagy
Anthony Neilsen (two volumes)
Philip Osment
Gary Owen
Louise Page
Stewart Parker (two volumes)
Joe Penhall (two volumes)
Stephen Poliakoff
  (three volumes)
David Rabe (two volumes)
Mark Ravenhill (two volumes)
Christina Reid
Philip Ridley
Willy Russell
Eric-Emmanuel Schmitt
Ntozake Shange
Sam Shepard (two volumes)
Wole Soyinka (two volumes)
Simon Stephens (two volumes)
Shelagh Stephenson
David Storey (three volumes)
Sue Townsend
Judy Upton
Michel Vinaver
  (two volumes)
Arnold Wesker (two volumes)
Michael Wilcox
Roy Williams (three volumes)
Snoo Wilson (two volumes)
David Wood (two volumes)
Victoria Wood

Methuen Drama Classical Greek Dramatists

Aeschylus Plays: One
(Persians, Seven Against Thebes, Suppliants,
Prometheus Bound)

Aeschylus Plays: Two
(Oresteia: Agamemnon, Libation-Bearers, Eumenides)

Aristophanes Plays: One
(Acharnians, Knights, Peace, Lysistrata)

Aristophanes Plays: Two
(Wasps, Clouds, Birds, Festival Time, Frogs)

Aristophanes & Menander: New Comedy
(Women in Power, Wealth, The Malcontent,
The Woman from Samos)

Euripides Plays: One
(Medea, The Phoenician Women, Bacchae)

Euripides Plays: Two
(Hecuba, The Women of Troy, Iphigeneia at Aulis,
Cyclops)

Euripides Plays: Three
(Alkestis, Helen, Ion)

Euripides Plays: Four
(Elektra, Orestes, Iphigeneia in Tauris)

Euripides Plays: Five
(Andromache, Herakles' Children, Herakles)

Euripides Plays: Six
(Hippolytos, Suppliants, Rhesos)

Sophocles Plays: One
(Oedipus the King, Oedipus at Colonus, Antigone)

Sophocles Plays: Two
(Ajax, Women of Trachis, Electra, Philoctetes)